BEC

BECOMING A SELF BEFORE GOD

Critical Transformations

ROMNEY M. MOSELEY

Abingdon Press
Nashville

BECOMING A SELF BEFORE GOD:
Critical Transformation

This book is printed on recycled acid-free paper.

Library of Congress Cataloging-in-Publication Data

Moseley, Romney M., 1943–
   Becoming a self before God: critical transformations/Romney M.
Moseley.
      p. cm.
   Includes bibliographical references and index.
                     ISBN 0-687-02504-4 (alk. paper)
   1. Ethics. 2. Faith. 3. Conversion. 4. Psychology, Religious.
5. Self 6. Social psychology. I. Title.
BJ1031.M67   1991
248.2—dc20   91-9642

Unless otherwise noted, scripture quotations are from the New Revised
Standard Version of the Bible, copyrighted © 1989, by the Division of Christian
Education of the National Council of the Churches of Christ in the United States
of America, and are used by permission.
   Excerpt from "Thinking About the God of the Poor: Questions for Liberation
Theology from Process Thought" by Delwin Brown is from *Journal of the
American Academy of Religion* 57 (Summer 1989), p. 273.

To Julia Marisa
God's gift to my own becoming

CONTENTS

CONTENTS

PREFACE

M any persons whose ideas and friendship sustained me through the writing of this book will not be mentioned. They include students and colleagues with whom I have had significant conversations on issues central to this book. To all of you and those mentioned below, I owe eternal gratitude.

I was fortunate to serve on the faculty of Candler School of Theology, Emory University, with several colleagues who were friends from my graduate student years at Harvard. Steve Tipton, David Pacini, Rex Matthews, and Carol Newsom continued a rich and noble tradition of scholarship and camaraderie. Richard Bondi, Ted Hackett, Luther Smith, Bob Perry, Mark Sciegaj, Charles Gerkin, and Rodney Hunter provided wise counsel on matters of the heart and mind that are indelibly etched in this book. Gail O'Day, Clinton Gardiner, and Catherine Meeks suggested helpful bibliographical resources. James Fowler, Mary Lou McCrary, and members of the Center for Research in Moral and Faith Development stimulated my ideas on moral and religious transformation. Anne Russell Mayeaux read early drafts of two chapters, and invited me to present them as papers at regional meetings of the American Academy of Religion. My former Dean, Jim L. Waits, granted me leave from my teaching and administrative responsibilities to write. The Houghton Library of Harvard University provided access to material on William James.

I would not have been able to write this book without the meticulous bibliographical research and critical insights of two doctoral students, Ernest Carrere and Brian Barlow.

Peter Slater and Joanne McWilliam, colleagues in the Faculty of Divinity, Trinity College, the University of Toronto, clarified some of my muddled thoughts on kenotic christology and transcendence. In the last days of trying to acquire new computer skills, the compassionate and merciful One sent me an angel of mercy, Darshan Dhillon.

Davis Perkins provided editorial direction at the inception of this project. Rex Matthews kept this project alive. My editor, Ulrike Guthrie, gave invaluable advice. Her patience throughout the production of the manuscript was an act of supererogation. Steve Cox and the editorial staff of Abingdon Press enriched the final draft significantly.

This book bears the marks of profound changes in the dialectic of struggle and surrender in my own life. In bringing it to completion, I came to appreciate, more and more, loved ones who created a space for me to recover a self that was in danger of being utterly consumed by a spiraling vortex of apocalyptic confusion. Not least among these loved ones are my wife, Joan Miriam, and daughter, Julia Marisa.

Trinity College
University of Toronto
All Saints Day, 1990

INTRODUCTION

In the sixties and early seventies, pedestrians in Harvard Square were fair game for the proselytizing of born again "Jesus freaks" and devotees of gurus, swamis, and other pundits from the Orient. American culture was in the midst of a religious awakening. New countercultural modes of being in the world attracted followers from all walks of life.

Armed with Lawrence Kohlberg's theory of moral development, I investigated various patterns in the structure of moral reasoning. James Fowler's theory of faith development provided a novel hermeneutical strategy for mapping transformations in cognitive and psychosocial dimensions of religious conversion. Given their basis in constructivist or structural-developmental psychology, both theories place the burden of moral development on a person's ability to achieve new levels of equilibrium as internal cognitive forces respond to environmental data.

The concept of faith as the structuring of meaning rests on the achievement of cognitive and psychosocial equilibrium in the relationship between the self and a transcendent center or centers of meaning and value. Stages of moral and faith development delineate the cognitive and psychosocial processes by which new forms of self-understanding are composed.

In the early years of applying stage theories to moral and religious development, I was primarily concerned with the empirical verification of the stages. In retrospect, I should have paid more attention to their metaphoric character and to the role of paradox in developmental theories. An analysis of metaphor and paradox prevents us from settling for the scientistic and empiricistic reductionism of closed systems of moral and religious development. Closed systems of moral and religious development fail to appreciate the hard paradoxes of faith as evidenced in the struggle to affirm meaning in the face of meaninglessness, doubt, suffering, and despair. Locked in a tunnel vision of linear progression and hierarchical stages, the moral life and religious faith fall victim to progressivism and triumphalism.

This was brought home to me rather forcefully some years ago in a conference on moral and faith development when one of the participants was quick to assign a woman's narrative of her struggle with painful aspects of her life to a stage of faith development normally characteristic of children. The artificial cognitive-developmental distinction between structure and content reinforced the devaluation of the painful content of this woman's story on the grounds of her apparent lack of sophisticated cognitive skills.

It is not difficult for theories of moral and religious development to succumb to the distortions of triumphalist ideologies and to relegate faith from the underside of history to the lowest levels of cognitive development. Triumphalist ideologies ignore the history of suffering and the eschatological hope for divine justice and freedom maintained by victims of oppression.

Given the North American obsession with triumphalism in its many forms, it is not surprising that pragmatism and its ally developmentalism are attractive hermeneutical strategies for charting moral and religious transformation. Both thrive on the myth of progress—in the case of pragmatism, a myth steeped in the American ethos of Promethean individualism; in the case of developmentalism, a neo-Hegelian myth of autonomous reason. In either case, morality and religion are filtered through a value system in which the hard paradoxes of faith are overcome by advancing through hierarchically ordered stages of moral and religious development.

My primary objective in this book is to provide a critique of developmentalism and triumphalism in contemporary North American religious life. My critique calls for two postures, one toward life itself and the other toward God. The first requires an appreciation of the hard paradoxes of faith—the struggle to affirm meaning in the face of meaninglessness, doubt, suffering, and despair. The acceptance of paradox is necessary for coping with the forces that threaten to undermine and negate authentic selfhood. This argument is supported by anthropologists who have studied cultures that are characterized by their appreciation for ambiguity and paradox.[1] The second posture requires an open-ended relationship to God in which new experiences of the ambiguity and plurality of divine revelation may be apprehended.

Chapter 1 examines James' phenomenology of religious faith and the moral life. James inherited the Puritan tradition of seeing suffering as a chastening rod for the cultivation of the moral life. Through the metaphor of the "strenuous mood," he describes the combined efforts of ethical individualism and cultural progress in nineteenth-century America, a period of profound religious awakening. The paradox of struggle and surrender is lost in the idealism of moral progress and the empiricism of Darwinian evolutionism. The future of the moral life rests with those at the vanguard of progress, the fittest exemplars of the strenuous mood, who in struggling to cultivate the moral life became victims of "neurasthenia" or nervous exhaustion.

In chapter 2, I explore the affinity between pragmatism and James Fowler's theory of faith development. The theology and ethics of H. Richard Niebuhr serve as the matrix of this relationship. Many of the problems arising from Fowler's theory stem from his incorporation of metaphysical claims about the self-transcendent relationship into a Piagetian empiricist framework. In the fusion of empiricism and idealism, the dialectic of *telos* and *eschaton* in the religious transformation of the self is lost in a web of structural stages of meaning-making and idealist visions of a post-paradoxical "synthetic" logic of "faith-knowing."

I argue that Fowler has not paid sufficient attention to the logic of paradox. This is crucial to the task of rescuing the theory of faith development from the passionless prison of constructivist psychology. In faith development theory, meaning-

13

making involves fitting opposites into a structured or coherent whole, specifically, the relationship between the self and a transcendent center of meaning and value. Progress from stage to stage leads to a widening of horizons of meaning, as conflicting and contradictory perspectives on the relationship between the self and the transcendent are integrated. Unfortunately, the Piagetian cognitive emphasis in faith development theory subsumes the paradoxes of the relationship between the self and the transcendent under the empiricist logic of physical reality.

In chapter 3, I propose an alternative to Fowler's structural-developmental paradigm. Drawing on dialectical psychology, I argue that human development is grounded in the multidimensionality and plurality of reality. The transformation of the self is a response to multiple arenas of conflict and ambiguity. Dialectical psychology advocates a continuing dialogue with the world—a questioning and reinterpreting of the multidimensionality of reality. This focus on how problems are generated and questions revised contrasts sharply with the problem-solving emphasis of Piagetian developmental psychology. In a nutshell, dialectical psychology is concerned with social dialectics—the changing relationship between a changing self and a changing world. In this dialectic of continuity and discontinuity in the self-world relationship, we encounter the tentativeness of change, the open-endedness and systemic nature of reality. Dialectical psychologists therefore refuse to map our knowing of the world as a sequence of hierarchically ordered stages. They press for a critique of ideology, including the ideology of the dialectical paradigm. The door remains open for novelty and the unexpected.

Dialectical psychology may be considered a hermeneutic of suspicion in questioning the perceptions of tranquility and balance in human development. In demythologizing stages of development, dialectical psychologists perform a task similar to that of theologians who are attempting to demythologize postmodern myths of progress. I consider the dialectical psychological paradigm of transformation an ally in my effort to preserve the historical conditioning of Christianity and its openness to otherness.

The idea of openness to otherness is further explored in

chapter 4 on Jung's analytical psychology. Jung's interpretation of the paradoxical structure of reality has important implications for the transformation of religious consciousness. His arguments for the individuation of wholeness as a paradox, a *mysterium coniunctionis* that can only be mediated symbolically, illumine the multidimensionality of religious experience. Jung charts human becoming as the anticipation of novelty and mystery. He anchors the numinosity (*sensus numinis*) of religious experience in the process of becoming a self, a fully individuated human being. The sense of otherness is at the heart of becoming whole. Jung is not a theologian but he stands in the numinous tradition of theological thought, which includes Schleiermacher, Otto, and Tillich. Jung's paradoxical hermeneutic enlarges the vistas of wholeness beyond the onesidedness of ego consciousness.

The problem with Jung is that paradox can easily dissolve into confusion as the transformations of the psyche become lost in a web of conflicting definitions of archetypes and wholeness becomes an idealized and idolatrous unity. In his desire to bring the forces of nature in the human personality and in the world under a single divine totality and to lodge the wholeness in the unfolding of God, Jung pays little attention to the tragic distortions of the *imago Dei* that result from human sin.

A more incisive analysis of the polarities and oppositions of paradox in the formation of Christian discipleship is given by Kierkegaard. Kierkegaard is a master of suspicion. He opposes the Kantian captivity of faith in a prison bounded by the limits of reason alone and rejects the Hegelian diachronic transformation of religious consciousness. While structural-developmentalists settle for the teleological ordering of reality, and Jungians for a *mysterium coniunctionis*, Kierkegaard cleaves to the hard paradoxes of existence—hope and despair, suffering and redemption, faith and doubt, the temporal and the eternal, the absence and presence of God.

Steeped in the intellectual ethos of Hegelian philosophy and the religious climate of Danish Lutheranism, Kierkegaard used his intellect as if it were a surgeon's scalpel to separate Christianity from the dross of Christendom. By plumbing the depths of existential despair and disclosing the paradoxes of

15

existence and of Christianity, Kierkegaard questions the authenticity of our identity as witnesses to the truth of Christianity. He refuses to settle for trite declarations of moral rectitude or religious rebirth. The paradoxes of existence militate against an optimistic reliance on culture and on inner spiritual resources for achieving any lasting experience of self-integration. The continuing transformation of the self is dictated by the dialectic of constancy and change in the formation of the self. This dialectic is dramatized by the concept of *repetition (Gjentagelsen)*.

Chapter 5 focuses on repetition as a metaphor for the dialectical transformation of the self as it experiences the aesthetic, ethical, and religious spheres of existence. Repetition is paradoxically a kairotic moment of passionate decisiveness to recover, literally to "retake" the past, and a kinetic movement toward a *vita ventura*—a life that is yet to come. In short, repetition eventuates from our willingness to let the past become the present and the present to be transformed not only by the past but by the future. Repetition dramatizes the loss and regaining of the self. *c.f. Eckhart*

Kairos

Each sphere of existence reflects the individual's struggle to bring the temporal values upon which the self is based into a deeper relationship to the eternal. The question for Kierkegaard is not the actualization of the meaning-making propensities of the self but the *authenticity of the self in the* face of the existential condition of suffering and despair. Kierkegaard is suspicious of the possibility of successfully mediating the hard paradoxical truths of the divine-human relationship embodied in the Incarnation and the moral paradoxes of the Crucifixion which thrust us into the despair of becoming a self before God.

Faith arises not out of the quest for meaning but from our "coming into existence," that is, from the reality that authentic selfhood is constituted only in relation to the infinite—namely, God. Faith comes to us as grace in our finitude. Without it, we drift like flotsam and jetsam in a world of vacuous aesthetic possibilities and conflicting moral demands. It is the abiding anchor that keeps us alive and in a state of death. In a nutshell, faith is a "happy passion." It is a surrendering to the Eternal, an act that inevitably places the Christian in the belly of paradox.

Kierkegaard's analysis of repetition calls for critical reflection on the dynamics of formation and imitation in Christian discipleship. The message of repetition is that God has not yet finished forming us in the image of God. To be retaken and re-formed by God is a scary prospect, for it means that we live on the boundary of the finite and the infinite. In this state of vulnerability and fragility, we are tempted to cling to the finite, to what is immediately fulfilling and self-affirming. We are also tempted to resort to the will, as if by mere strenuous moral effort we could appropriate the *imago Dei* into the structure of our psyches.

Kierkegaard underscores the paradox of resoluteness—the decisiveness of the will as we strive to be like Christ and the spirit of surrendering to the transforming power of God. This is demonstrated in the divine self-emptying or *kenosis* of Christ.

The *kenosis* of Christ is the christological matrix of this book. There is no place in kenoticism for Promethean individualism or religious triumphalism. A kenotic theology of Christian becoming shifts the axis of the moral life away from the achievements of the autonomous subject toward anamnestic solidarity with victims. It infuses our accomplishments and successes with the awesome pain of God in the humiliation of Christ. These arguments are set forth in chapter 6.

The kenotic paradigm brings us full circle. Having begun with the strenuous mood and its strident efforts to empower the moral life, it is fitting that I conclude by reflecting on the paradoxical empowerment of the Church as it lives out its faith in God whose power is perfected in weakness. The recovery of paradoxical knowing in the Church will result not only in the dethroning of triumphalism and privatism but also in the decentering of Christianity.

I am intrigued by Tom Driver's observation that we are living in an Einsteinian universe in which no one system of values is absolute, and in which it makes no sense to speak of christocentrism.[2] Driver is an inscrutable religious pluralist who wants Christians to view the truth claims of Christianity as part of a pluralistic universe in which all systems of organization and understanding have a legitimate autonomy. This is a troublesome proposition for Christians who ground their identity and faith in an impenetrable fortress of christocentrism where the Christ who is to be imitated and obeyed is a protector against the ambiguity and plurality of religious life.

The massive restructuring of cultural life throughout the world, for example in Europe and South Africa, forces us to examine existing paradigms of moral and religious transformation in the Church as the body of Christ. Though I do not fully agree with Driver's interpretation of Christ on the basis of Einstein's theory of relativity, I am convinced that Christians need to be prodded away from christocentrism toward a present and future in which the relativity of Christianity to other religions and to the history of the world is acknowledged.

The drift of Driver's argument is that Christians should be less interested in preserving Christianity as an unchangeable bulwark in the midst of a changing world and more concerned about discovering who Christ is in a world that is undergoing radical cultural transformations. If, as Driver argues, the Christ of the New Testament is oriented to the future, then the Christian vocation is to live on the horizon of new beginnings and possibilities.

A paradoxical vision of reality is necessary for living out this concept of the Christian vocation. Christianity is both a recollection of the salvation history of God in Christ and an orienting of the present to a life that is yet to come. Given this paradox, it is easy to encapsulate Christ in a fixed moral universe of pious souls who have become "born again" for all time, or to have Christ mimic a carefully manicured and sanitized culture of success and progress, or to imprison Christ in a totalitarian structure of ecclesiastical authority.

Fortunately, the Church universal is experiencing a reformation of its identity and mission, thanks to the impetus of grassroots liberation theologies in Latin America, Africa, and Asia. These narratives of freedom and justice disclose the relativity and risk of Christian discipleship and apostleship in a changing world. They invite all who profess to be baptized into the death and resurrection of Jesus Christ to risk being transformed by God's self-emptying love. I believe that these testimonies are fruits of the Holy Spirit.

CHAPTER ONE

RELIGIOUS FAITH AND THE MORAL LIFE

For the past two decades theologians, ethicists, philosophers, and social scientists have been paying considerable attention to the relationship between the shaping of the moral self and that of public life. Martin Marty notes that personal conversion is inextricably linked to the transformative praxis of the public church.[1] Parker Palmer suggests that the renewal of public life is a "ministry of paradox" since it demands an intensification of the inward journey of faith as well as effective public action.[2] Robert Bellah and his colleagues conclude that the transformation of American culture requires a reconnecting of radical individualism and public life.[3]

Liberation theologians are also protesting the alienation that results from the gulf between the interior self and public life. They challenge the privatization of the self, the self-world dualism, and they question the legitimacy of treating religious faith and the moral life apart from the socio-historical setting of human existence.

Much of the contemporary discussion on the need for integrating religious faith and the moral life recapitulates arguments set forth by William James at the turn of the century. James addressed the fragmentation of the relationship between religious faith and the moral life from his dual interests in philosophy and psychology. His writings reflect a concerted effort to link moral athleticism in American life with the evolution of a moral universe. His ideas serve as a point of departure for my analysis of the more recent transformation of moral and religious life in North America.

At the outset, I must warn my readers that James' language is quite abstruse. He wrote at a time when psychology was emerging from philosophy as a distinct science. The movement back and forth between these two disciplines is not only reflected in his writings but is also evidenced by his movement between the departments of philosophy and psychology at Harvard. In order to explicate his ideas on religious faith and the moral life, it is necessary to delve into the intricacies of his thoughts on the concept of the self and its relation to the world. I intend to show that James is a moralist at heart and that he sees religion mainly as a resource for energizing the moral transformation of humanity.

1. James considered himself a radical empiricist, as opposed to a classical empiricist, such as Locke and Hume. Thus, he rejected the classical empiricist fragmentation of experience into a disparate mass of atomistic ideas and sensations. Instead, he argued that experience flowed like the flux or stream of consciousness in which continuity between the knower and the known is maintained and our attention becomes focused on what evokes our interests and satisfies our needs. In other words, the scope of our experience is continuously being expanded. Religious experience is a part of this stream of consciousness. The individual is connected to an ever widening stream of experience from which emanate concepts of the divine.

James defined religion as *"the feelings, acts, and experiences of individual men in their solitude, so far as they apprehend themselves to stand in relation to whatever they may consider the divine."*[4] What is apprehended as the divine does not exist apart from the general flux of experience. James is unwilling to attribute to the divine any absolute qualities that would infringe on human free will, for example omnipotence. His Darwinian leanings also made it difficult for him to accept divine interference in organic evolution. This resistance to absolutisms also extends to the moral life. And so James concentrates on the function of religious experience in the shaping of the moral life.

James also rejected the idealist argument for a trans-empirical form of cognition, for example, Kant's transcendental ego of apperception and Hegel's Absolute Spirit. Both maintained the epistemological dualism of mind and body. James maintained that consciousness was not an entity which existed as an ontologically distinct form of reality. Consciousness is to be understood in terms of its knowing function. By consciousness is meant to be conscious *of*, to be in relation *to* the world. Through consciousness, our experience of the world is organized into several functions, for example, the physical, spiritual, and psychical. All of these are related to one another as part of the same "primal stuff in the world," namely, undifferentiated "pure experience." Concepts such as subject and object are not ontologically discrete categories of cognition but are practical or functional distinctions between relative aspects of the same non-dualistic, primal experience.

It is important to bear in mind this functional approach to cognition. It holds together James' radical empiricism and pragmatism. Radical empiricism is concerned with the continuity of experience. Pragmatism is concerned with the verification of experience, its truth and meaning. As a pragmatist, James maintains a coherent theory of truth and meaning. Since there are no absolutes, truth is not verified by its correspondence to some a priori experience or absolute. Rather, it is verified by the coherence of its claims with other truths. In the marketplace of verification, no truth holds any a priori claim over another.

In the case of religion, pragmatism holds sway. The pragmatist stance that knowledge is a cooperative activity by which the world is ordered also applies to religious beliefs. Belief in God is simply one among many beliefs that contribute to the ordering of the world. As far as James was concerned, we need not argue whether or not God exists. More important is to describe the kind of personality embodying such a belief and the contributions of belief in God to the well-being of the world. The truths generated by belief in God are verified not by their correspondence to some established set of doctrines but by their coherence with other beliefs.

To summarize, religious experience is part of our lived experience. It is neither ontologically subjective nor objective.

Its reality is manifest in the concrete lives of persons. The uniqueness of religious experience is that it demonstrates our continuity with "a wider self through which saving experiences come." This connectedness with a wider self—"an Ideal Power"—is reflected in the character of "saintliness," "the character for which spiritual emotions are the habitual centre of the personal energy."[5]

RELIGIOUS CONVERSION

James' insistence on functional as opposed to ontological distinctions in our lived experience has important implications for his interpretation of religious conversion. The sudden or "instantaneous" conversions are evidence that consciousness brings into focus peripheral aspects of our lived experience. It is as though these volcanic eruptions eventuate from emotions that were dormant sometime. There is clear analogy to thermodynamics. Religious conversion is a concentration of energy in the subconscious.

> What makes the difference between a sudden and a gradual convert is not necessarily the presence of divine miracle in the case of one and of something less divine in that of the other, but rather a simple psychological peculiarity, the fact, namely, that in the recipient of the more instantaneous grace we have one of those subjects who are in possession of a large region in which mental work can go on subliminally, and from which invasive experiences, abruptly upsetting the equilibrium of the primary consciousness, may come.

> I do indeed believe that if the subject have no liability to such subconscious activity, or if his conscious fields have a hard rind of a margin that resists incursions from beyond it, his conversion must be gradual if it occur, and must resemble any simple growth into new habits. His possession of a developed subliminal self, and of a leaky or pervious margin, is thus a *conditio sine qua non* of the subject's being converted in the instantaneous way.[6]

A whole new way of being in the world eventuates from the conversion experience. Specifically, the conversion experience integrates the divided self—a self fragmented by sin. It also demonstrates the moral relationship between the self and the world. The moral transformation of the self not only is accomplished on the level of interiority (through the unification of the divided self), but also entails moral action on the world. In other words, the formation of the moral self is to be understood both actively and passively. "The self [is] transforming, but the self [is] also transformed."[7]

James was aware that persons experience integration of self in a variety of ways, not only toward but also away from religiosity and morality. The alteration of a person's life from one direction to another or the abandonment of certain beliefs in favor of others does not constitute religious conversion. Rather, the significance of religious conversion is its enhancement of the moral life. The moral life does not need religion for its legitimation but religion needs the moral life for its legitimation. The burden is therefore on religion to be healthy, for healthy religion energizes the moral life, exposing it to its greatest challenges and taking it to its zenith by demanding self-sacrifice.

HEALTHY RELIGION AND THE STRENUOUS MOOD

James identified three aspects of the self, each according to specific functions of consciousness, namely, the material, social, and spiritual. The material self is the bodily self. The social self refers to the images of ourselves in the minds of others—the *persona* we assume in interpersonal relationships. These two aspects of the self, the material and the social, constitute the *empirical* self—the observable "me." In addition, there is the *spiritual* self—the "self of all other selves."[8] John Wild points out that the spiritual self "is not an object referred *to*." It is "the inner citadel of selfhood," and does not "exist" apart from the embodied empirical self.[9]

In reflecting on the moral and religious transformation of the self, James is careful to describe the self as an integrated complex of mind, body, and spirit. His metaphor for the moral life is the "strenuous mood." This is a combination of willpower, persistence, and moral discernment. It depicts the self actively engaged in the creation of a moral universe.

> The deepest difference, practically, in the moral life of man is the difference between the easy-going and the strenuous mood. When in the easy-going mood the shrinking from present ill is our ruling consideration. The strenuous mood, on the contrary, makes us quite indifferent to present ill, if only the greater ideal be attained. The capacity for the strenuous mood probably lies slumbering in every man, but it has more difficulty in some than in others in waking up. It needs the wilder passions to arouse it, the big fears, loves, and indignations; or else the deeply penetrating appeal of some of the higher fidelities, like justice, truth, or freedom.[10]

Furthermore, the strenuous mood is strengthened by and brought to its ultimate fulfillment by religious faith (practical theism).

> The capacity of the strenuous mood lies so deep down among our natural human possibilities that even if there were no metaphysical or traditional grounds for believing in a God, men would postulate one simply as a pretext for living hard, and getting out of the game of existence its keenest possibilities of zest. Our attitude towards concrete evils is entirely different in a world where we believe there are none but finite demanders, from what it is in one where we joyously face tragedy for an infinite demander's sake. Every sort of energy and endurance, of courage and capacity for handling life's evils, is set free in those who have religious faith. For this reason the strenuous type of character will on the battle-field of human history always outwear the easy-going type, and religion will drive irreligion to the wall.[11]

According to Don Browning, the strenuous mood is "simultaneously mystical, ethical, and heroic."[12] It is mystical in that it is the surrender of the self to the ever-changing and ever-widening spiritual center of reality from which saving experiences emanate. Here James' panpsychism is apparent. It is ethical in its resistance to philosophical monism, which minimizes the reality of evil by incorporating it into a perfected, unalterable, and all-embracing whole. Such an attitude toward

24

life encourages passivity and vitiates any impetus for genuine moral transformation. The strenuous mood is also heroic in that the individual is struggling against determinism and nihilism. Altogether, the strenuous mood cultivates the making of moral choices that are genuinely self-sacrificial.

The strenuous mood is James' way of integrating the ethics of character, the religious affections, and social praxis. To live in the strenuous mood is to be engaged in the task of moral and spiritual transformation. Here, stoical resistance to the vicissitudes of life, though helpful for some persons in their defiance of fate, does not evoke the kind of moral and spiritual transformation demanded by belief in God. Belief in God brings the strenuous mood to its fullest expression. By believing in God our values are placed in an ultimate frame of reference and our moral striving takes on infinite possibility.

> This too is why, in a merely human world without a God, the appeal to our moral energy falls short of its maximal stimulating power. Life, to be sure, is even in such a world a genuinely ethical symphony; but it is played in the compass of a couple of poor octaves, and the infinite scale of values fails to open up.

> When, however, we believe that a God is there, and that he is one of the claimants, the infinite perspective opens out. The scale of the symphony is incalculably prolonged. The more imperative ideals now begin to speak with an altogether new objectivity and significance, and to utter the penetrating, shattering, tragically challenging note of appeal.[13]

In other words, the differences between nonbelievers and believers are analogous to differences between a few bars in a musical piece and a full symphony. Through belief in God our humanity is brought to its fullest expression. Without it, there is no genuine engagement with the reality of evil in the world; without it, conversion has no ultimate *telos* or universal significance.

James' account of practical theism has important implications for the quality of religion in the world. Healthy religion evokes the strenuous mood and unhealthy religion dulls our sensitivity to the profundity of evil. Ironically, James is critical of the "religion of healthy-mindedness" propagated by the "mind-curists" and other philosophical monists who consider evil to be a matter of the suggestibility of the mind, hence define healthy religion as the absence of evil. The religion of healthy-mindedness stands in sharp contrast to that of the "morbid-minded" or the "sick soul" for whom evil is not merely an intellectual problem but is a debilitating and tortuous experience. It is the sick soul that experiences conversion as spiritual rebirth.

> To this latter way, the morbid-minded way, as we might call it, healthy-mindedness pure and simple seems unspeakably blind and shallow. To the healthy-minded way, on the other hand, the way of the sick soul seems unmanly and diseased. With their grubbing in rat-holes instead of living in the light; with their manufacture of fears, and pre-occupation with every unwholesome kind of misery, there is something almost obscene about these children of wrath and cravers of second birth.[14]

Eventually, James adopts a middle position between the religion of the once-born and that of the twice-born. In *The Varieties of Religious Experience,* he expresses a strong affection for the sick soul or twice-born. Later in "The Energies of Men," in *Pragmatism,* and in *A Pluralistic Universe,* he is attracted to the strident self-confidence and belief in the betterment of life (meliorism) held by the healthy-minded or once-born.[15] On the one hand, the sick soul's preoccupation with evil and sinfulness encourages escapism into a private self. On the other hand, in minimizing the concreteness of evil, the once-born eliminate the necessity of repentance and conversion, thereby undermining the strenuous mood.

James adopts a middle position between the meliorism of healthy-mindedness and the sick soul's emphasis on conversion. In this position, he focuses on conversions that evoke the multiple energies of the will, intellect, and religious affections. He postulates that religious conversion may be a means of lifting persons to higher levels of moral energy and therefore disclosing new options for the strenuous mood.

In light of the above, one could easily identify James with religious triumphalism. The latter is seen today in such forms as "possibility thinking" and "positive thinking." But these are aberrations of the strenuous mood. James would argue that the single most important task for the religious convert is to apply the newly released moral energy to the benefit of the common good, for example, through education and the promotion of democracy.

James did not advocate escape into a private self. Although the strenuous mood refers to the formation of a particular type of moral character, it is not a singleminded striving for moral rectitude or an obsessive appetite for success in competitive American society. Rather, it is a manifestation of the interconnectedness of the moral self and the common good.[16] As such, it incorporates the cardinal elements of James' moral philosophy: (1) intimate connection of the self to a wider reservoir of experience; (2) the human capacity for creating new possibilities for a meaningful life; (3) resistance to determinism—"the most pernicious and immoral of fatalisms."[17]

In summary, James' picture of the strenuous mood (the moral life) complements his vision of American culture at the helm of human development. The moral life is a combination of ethical individualism and civic virtue. Its ingredients cover a wide span of personal and cultural values—"fidelity, cohesiveness, tenacity, heroism, conscience, education, inventiveness, economy, wealth, physical health and vigor."[18] The strenuous mood is not for the faint of heart. Neurasthenia (nervous exhaustion) is a likely affliction. Neurasthenia enervates the initiatives of inventors, the creativity of geniuses, and general cultural progress. Hence James advocated occasional "moral holidays."[19]

One would think that religious institutions would be at the vanguard of the cultivation of the moral life. Not so for James. James is more confident that educational institutions will do a better job. As far as he is concerned, one of the primary goals of education is democracy. And democracy is the moral matrix of American society. It allows those at the bottom of the social ladder to share in the same ideals of those at the top. It ensures that ethical individualism does not degenerate into egoistic utilitarianism. It is left then to religious institutions to get on board the moral wagon. At least, the moral consequences of religious conversions offer some hope that religious institutions are involved in widening the moral landscape.

But is it enough to rest the moral life on the cooperative ventures of strenuous living and democracy? James is convinced that America is at the helm of the evolution of goodness. Through its moral consciousness, the perfecting of the world is mediated. But what about justice and freedom? James assumes that democracy guarantees both. Democracy is a result of mutual social perspective-taking. The self is a social self, part of a wider common life. Democracy ensures that each individual is free to direct his or her energies toward the common good and to be a beneficiary of the common good. This idea of relationships fitting together in a common moral matrix is the heart of James' coherent theory of truth and value. In the following chapter, I will show how this ideal is carried forth in faith development theory. Before turning to this matter, I need to say something more about James' concept of God.

PRACTICAL THEISM AND PLURALISTIC PANTHEISM

James follows Kant in affirming the *praxis* of ethical decisiveness. Practical reason ensures decisive willing and believing. As a pragmatist, James is also concerned about the impact of beliefs on conduct, especially beliefs concerning ultimate meaning. A natural characteristic of being human is to question the ultimate meaning of life. Such questioning is part of our moral consciousness. For James, "the radical question of life" is not whether God exists but "whether this be at bottom a moral or an unmoral universe."[20]

Belief in God is an "overbelief," that is, a belief for which there is no logical proof but which is nonetheless useful in shaping the moral life. James asserts that "we and God have business with each other; and in opening ourselves to his influence our deepest destiny is fulfilled. . . . God is real since he produces real effects."[21] This is the essence of practical theism. The principal function of religious belief is to sustain an uncompromising optimism regarding the "organic and intimate" presence of the divine in the world.

God's existence is the guarantee of an ideal order that shall be permanently preserved. This world, may indeed, as science assures us, some day burn up or freeze; but if it is part of his order, that where God is, tragedy is only provisional and partial, and shipwreck and dissolution are not absolutely final things.[22]

The belief that persons are intimate partners with God in the perfecting of the world leaves unlimited possibility for moral action, from the simplest to the sublime. Democratic ideals require mutual social perspective-taking if the common good is to be served. No less is expected of God. Moreover, James found in Darwinian evolutionary theory a clear case for the organic and intimate role of divine involvement in the perfecting of the universe.

It is evident that James does not articulate the presence of God in human history in terms of the Christian concept of the Incarnation. God's intimacy with the universe is mediated in multiple ways, all of which are available to human experience, thereby affording "a higher degree of intimacy."[23] Practical theism is couched in a larger framework of pluralistic pantheism.

All indications are that religion, specifically belief in God and religious conversion, widens the horizons of moral transformation beyond the ethical individualism of the strenuous mood. Most important, the conscious striving to improve the moral life comes up against the profound paradox of surrendering to a power greater than the self. James does not abandon his view of God as coworker, but there is a clear sense that God is a power greater than the conscious self. The issue here is the meeting of will and spirit.

The image of the individual struggling to do the good and the right in cooperation with an equally driven God is undoubtedly appropriate for some persons. For such persons, the entirety of the divine-human relationship is consumed with obedience to the will of God. James wants us to consider also the mystical aspect of the divine-human relationship. Mystical union is a paradigm of the paradox of struggle and surrender in the divine-human relationship. It is a distinctive form of spiritualism, namely, dualistic theism, which is predicated on the separation of the human and the divine and the surrender of the human to the divine. From James' point of view, more than any other religious personalities mystics recognize that when the strenuousness of moral striving is combined with spiritualism, the center of gravity of moral transformation shifts from struggle to surrender.

Though not a theologian, James concludes that letting go to this greater power is "psychologically indistinguishable from the Lutheran justification by faith and the Wesleyan acceptance of free grace."[24] In other words, denominational affiliation has nothing to do with this paradox. Letting go "is within the reach of persons who have no conviction of sin and care nothing for the Lutheran theology. It is but giving your little private convulsive self a rest, and finding that a greater Self is there."[25] Without this attitude of surrender we are left with the tensions and suspicions of "materialism." Spiritualism encourages us to "give way, embrace, and keep no ultimate fear."[26] The "greater Self" is there for all to experience. Truths eventuating from this experience of God are to be tested in the community of public discourse. In a pluralistic universe, there is always some other facet of reality to be discovered.

> Things are 'with' one another in many ways, but nothing includes everything, or dominates over everything. The word 'and' trails along after every sentence. Something always escapes. 'Ever not quite' has to be said of the best attempts made anywhere in the universe at attaining all-inclusiveness. The pluralistic world is thus more like a federal republic than like an empire or a kingdom.[27]

SALVATION AND THE INTEGRATED SELF

We have then from James a broad view of the quest for moral and religious meaning. James considered himself a meliorist—one who believes that there is an underlying spiritual reality to material existence which invigorates the continuing moral and religious transformation of the world. He defines salvation as the integration of our material and spiritual selves. This is not a predestined but is a *probable* outcome of the cooperative

30

divine-human relationship. James has no respect for an absolute God—a *deus absconditus* who leaves human beings to sort out their own salvation with fear and trembling. Nor is he attracted to the "monarchical theism" of Calvinism. Simply put, for James, the salvation of the world benefits both God and the world.

As far as James is concerned, salvation is a "faith-state" or "working hypothesis" which stands to be verified. Stated differently, the salvation of the world is necessary for legitimating belief in God. The more pious among us will certainly be offended by this affront to God's omnipotence. Even more disturbing is James' assertion that the task of saving the world is too big for God alone to handle. In response, we could say that this problem was taken care of by God in becoming incarnate in Jesus Christ. The Incarnation is not just a revelation of God's willingness to cooperate with humanity but is an act of God's self-emptying love for humanity.

This *kenosis* is recapitulated again on the cross. In a word, the crux of the divine-human relation is not *power* but *love*. Salvation therefore is not centered on whether God is omnipotent or less than omnipotent but on God's love for the world in spite of human sin. The matter of cooperation with God makes sense, but this drama is not played out as an exercise in power-sharing but in the mutual *kenosis* of God and humanity—God's self-emptying and humanity's surrender.[28] This is not a one-shot deal but a continuing process. Hence, to proclaim that one is "saved" should not be a statement of closure on a task completed; it should be a declaration that one is intimately involved in a process of moral and religious transformation, the final outcome of which is unknown.

At a time when competing constituencies in American religious life seek dominance over one another and salvation is being packaged through the broadcast media as a private commodity, I find James' pluralistic pantheism rather refreshing. He envisions a genuine public arena in which salvation is understood as a cooperative goal for all persons, without any guarantee of its inevitability. This demands an increasing development of moral responsibility as each person assumes a role in transforming salvation from an "unseen reality" into an observable "affectional fact," that is, lived experience. Salvation history is not limited to the integration of "divided selves" but is inextricably linked to the formation of social institutions whose *raison d'être* is to satisfy the demand for the right and the good.

SAINTLINESS AND THE MORAL LIFE

Having declared that salvation is not an accomplished reality but a cooperative venture for those willing to take on the strenuous life, it follows that we should at least note some examples of persons who illumine this perspective. For James, these are the world transformers who embody the virtues of saintliness. "The collective name for the ripe fruits of religion in a character is Saintliness."[29] Saintliness is exemplified by such "superhuman founders" of religions as "the Christ, the Buddha and Mahomet."[30] These "religious geniuses" have had "original experiences" in contrast to the "second-hand religious life" of the "ordinary religious believer," whose religion "has been made for him by others, communicated to him by tradition, determined to fixed forms by imitation, and retained by habit."[31]

Saintliness sets the moral standards for the rest of humanity. Among its salient features are:

> 1. A feeling of being in a wider life than that of this world's selfish little interests; and a conviction, not merely intellectual, but as it were sensible, of the existence of an Ideal Power. . . .
> 2. A sense of the friendly continuity of the ideal power with our own life, and a willing self-surrender to its control.
> 3. An immense elation and freedom, as the outlines of the confining selfhood melt down.
> 4. A shifting of the emotional centre towards loving and harmonious affections, towards "yes, yes," and away from "no," where the claims of the non-ego are concerned.[32]

These fundamental traits give rise to other moral dispositions such as "asceticism, strength of soul, blissful equanimity, purity, and charity."[33] Of these, asceticism epitomizes the strenuous mood:

> For in its spiritual meaning asceticism stands for nothing less than for the essence of the twice-born philosophy. It symbolizes,

lamely enough no doubt, but sincerely, the belief that there is an element of real wrongness in this world, which is neither to be ignored nor evaded, but which must be squarely met and overcome by an appeal to the soul's heroic resources, and neutralized and cleansed away by suffering.[34]

Though he rejects ordinary religious beliefs and rituals, James appeals to stereotypical characteristics of the religious personality. Religious beliefs eventuate from religious attitudes or dispositions that are formed in religious experience. Each variety of religious experience generates its own particular attitude toward the ultimate questions of existence. Hence belief in God, that is, in "any object that is god*like,* whether it be a concrete deity or not,"[35] evokes a peculiar attitude of solemnity and strenuousness.

In spite of his insistence on religious pluralism, James settled for a superficial and culturally biased view of the religious personality. He denigrated the "hindoo and the buddhist" for seeking nirvana, which he believed was an escape from the strenuous mood.[36] Persons of this "complexion" were religious monists who simply surrendered to oneness with God. They lacked guts. He favored toughminded religions that faced up to the problem of suffering. Unfortunately, James was so wedded to typologies of religious experience that he placed considerable weight on linking personalities to types of religion.

James was neither a historian of religion nor a theologian. He was interested in extracting a common substance of theological discourse from the religious experiences of individuals. Theology was of secondary importance to religious experience. As a result, his theological ruminations are confusing and unsystematic.

EVIL, THEODICY, AND A FINITE GOD

It would seem from what I have explicated so far that James was not particularly interested in what kind of God persons believed in, so long as God did not subvert essential aspects of humanity, such as free will. Yet, James did not approve of atheism. He considered atheism to be just another form of absolutism comparable to determinism. God is the Ultimate, not the Absolute. This teleological reading of theology is consistent with his embrace of Darwinian evolutionism. In the course of evolution, order and stability are brought to a chaotic world. Evolution also brings novelty to the universe. The excitement generated by Darwinian evolutionary theory reinforced James' stance toward process theology. An omnipotent and omniscient God would be removed from the struggles and permutations of the universe but would also make human efforts to derive meaning in the world appear utterly trivial and insignificant.

Given this finite God, how does James account for theodicy? James acknowledges that evil is indeed a real problem and we have to find pragmatic ways to soften its impact on life. However, this problem is not solved by an omnipotent God. On the contrary, an omnipotent God makes matters worse by giving rise to other metaphysical problems such as theodicy. James wants more of God's involvement in the affairs of the world and less of evil. But he does not explain the relation between God and evil. Pluralistic pantheism leaves the space open for God and humans to work toward the diminution of evil. Anything short of intimate cooperation means that God has willfully chosen to ignore the suffering of the innocent or is incapable of doing anything about it. James refuses to speculate on the absolute triumph of good over evil. He is more interested in the efforts of a loving God and of moral persons to alleviate evil. An omnipotent God who is in complete control of the world would eliminate not only evil but also freedom of will. Having freedom of will means that we have to experience genuine feelings of regret over our actions and choices. There is a proper sense of rightness and wrongness about our choices and actions. Thus the struggle to overcome evil is the onus of humans. Evil cannot simply be subsumed under the fiat of an omnipotent being.

James also took issue with those who saw in the Darwinian theory of natural selection a way out of confronting the moral demands of evil. To attribute evil to biological necessity was also a surrender to determinism. This encouraged individuals to disregard the imperatives of the strenuous life and society to deny its part in the shaping of moral values.

34

WIDENING THE MORAL HORIZONS

In the struggle to deal with evil, we are benefited by the examples of the "superhuman founders" of religions and other great exemplars of strenuous living. From them we learn that the moral transformation of persons and the salvation of the world are ideals worth striving for.

Each of us has to find ways of contributing to the salvation of the world. In nineteenth-century America, the standard route was religious conversion—a seminal moment in the salvation of the world. For the convert, the conversion experience sharpens the awareness of what is valuable and worth striving for in life. It invigorates persons to propagate the purposiveness of life and to be intensely engaged in making moral evaluations. In short, through religious conversion the personal and public dimensions of the moral life are integrated. As an individual, the convert has to make concrete decisions and follow through with moral commitments. Religious conversion also widens the moral horizon beyond ethics for the individual. With it comes commitment to a community of faith. Unfortunately, some converts become ideological fanatics. They feel compelled to display their rebirth, even if it means infringing on the beliefs of others.

Any system of interpretation can become ideological, including pragmatism, in spite of its objective to be a means of verification. James resists specifying any absolute moral goals and values. Moral goals and values are enacted in response to the demands of the human condition. The key to their worth is their ability to stand the test of time as satisfactory principles for ordering human life: how they help us make difficult decisions, resolve conflicts, organize social behavior, and so on. James assumes that social institutions and social life in general will evolve in such a way as to accommodate the demands of the common good. In other words, moral progress is inextricably linked to social progress.

By now, we should be suspicious of James' unbridled confidence in the evolution of moral consciousness. Nineteenth-century America promised unlimited social progress, and it exuded the necessary religious fervor to keep the moral fires burning until the millennium. Given this climate, it was natural for James to identify acts of commitment to social progress with moral virtue. Thus he defined love as self-sacrifice for the sake of others. As an example, he cited the conscription of able-bodied male college students to work on social welfare projects instead of training for war. Self-sacrifice cultivated by efforts such as these would eventually replace the need for war. Also included among the virtuous were mystics who, in surrendering to the divine, were empowered to give more of themselves to the moral and religious transformation of humanity. As a result, some mystics could even become saints.

Self-sacrifice, then, is the crucial point at which surrender to a greater Self and striving for the common good are united. In James' view, those for whom God is the greater Self are more driven to seek moral change for themselves and for the rest of the world. James' God is the ultimate moral demander—one who, persons believe, demands more of them morally than any existing human. The point is, the moral imperative of self-sacrifice does not arise from belief in God. For James, the moral fabric of the universe does not depend on God—neither on an absolute God who is removed from the vicissitudes of temporality nor on a finite God who is incapable of overcoming evil. Without God, we still have a fundamentally moral universe but, surely, one incapable of reaching its highest moral potential. However, when moral strenuousness is combined with belief in God as coworker in the moral vineyard, self-sacrifice takes on a whole new meaning.

James fails to plumb the theological significance of self-sacrifice. The ultimate test of divine self-sacrifice is God's submission to suffering and death. God's submission to suffering and death is not a matter of God's need for intimacy or sympathy with the human. God's suffering and death are consistent with God's self-emptying in the Creation and Incarnation. Each of these events is a paradox. The new life that is brought into being is eternal life, which, paradoxically, is both already present and not yet. This eschatological proviso makes relative the moralism of strenuousness. It is perhaps one of the "metaphysical paradoxes" James finds confusing to pragmatism. My theological sensibilities lead me to conclude that the salvation of the world is an "in spite of" experience rather than a cooperative divine-human venture. The kernel of grace is the enduring reality of God's love in spite of human sinfulness and the frailty of our efforts to love God.

In summary, James defines religious faith and the moral life in terms of an invisible power or greater Self that invigorates us to deal with moral conflict, evil, and tragedy. This is a cooperative enterprise that benefits both God and humanity. Working together, God and humans can transform the "half-wild, half-saved universe" into a universe that is "good for moral men."[37] This cooperative venture requires self-sacrifice by all, including God. Missing from this cooperative arrangement is a sense of vocation—that persons are called by God into a covenantal community of faith. The ethic of cooperation is teleologically grounded. Its objective is to widen the contours of the moral life by the convergence of divine and human will. A tacit agenda is to eliminate supernatural images of God. In contrast, a covenantal ethic rests on the willingness of persons to respond freely to the God who first called humanity into covenant in creation and continues to call humanity into new covenants. Implicit in this ethic are the ambiguities of sin and forgiveness and the paradoxes of striving and letting go.

This discussion of the covenantal ethic continues in chapter 2, on pragmatism and structuralism in James Fowler's theory of faith development.

CHAPTER TWO

DEVELOPMENTAL
TRANSFORMATIONS

Sometime ago, I met a woman who was utterly consumed by her recent "born again" experience. As is the case with many seminarians, this experience was taken to be an authentic sign of a divine call to enter the ordained ministry. Tessa had suffered a hard life in a ghetto in one of America's inner cities. She grew up surrounded by drugs, prostitution, poverty, and homicides. She was also steeped in the religious heritage of her ancestors. The black storefront church she attended as a child was a bastion of faith, hope, and love in a heartless world.

Tessa went off to college. She stopped attending church. She started taking hallucinogenic drugs. Not long afterward, she had a remarkable religious experience. In a hotel room one night with her lover, she saw Jesus. Yes, she gave her soul to Jesus that night and considered herself saved. She called her relatives and testified to the great and glorious deeds that Jesus had done for her. They were most delighted. They asked her to return home the next day. The local pastor was informed. Since the church was having a grand revival at the time, the pastor invited Tessa to testify before the church. She gladly complied and a good time was had by all.

Within a couple of months following this burst of religious fervor, Tessa discovered that she was pregnant. She had to make a decision—whether to tell her relatives that she had conceived during her ecstatic experience in the hotel room.

Would this invalidate her testimonies of rebirth and salvation? Should she leave town and have her child elsewhere without informing her relatives? Should she have an abortion? In the dark night of the soul when religious faith is overcome by doubt and moral certainty by utter confusion, what is the right thing to do? Tessa decided to have an abortion and to leave town. No more witnessing for God. No more testimonies of salvation. Her life moved in a different direction. Astrology, numerology, palmistry, and other occult ideas filled the void.

Sometime later, Tessa met up with a group of "new Christians" who took her under their wing. Once again, she surrendered to Christ and was born again. This time, seminary was the obvious place in which to explore her transformed existence.

Armed with Kohlberg's theory of moral reasoning and James Fowler's theory of faith development, I identified Tessa's stage of moral development as Stage Three "good boy-good girl" moral reasoning.[1] Decision making was on the basis of perceptions of goodness maintained by her peers. Nevertheless, I found Kohlberg's stages inadequate for dealing with the matter of religious faith. Kohlberg maintained a neo-Kantian approach to religion and morality. Religious faith functions within the limits of reason alone. Kohlberg's stages function as categories of moral reasoning within which the rational contents of religious faith are located.

Fowler's theory of faith development proved more helpful.[2] This theory incorporates a modified version of Kohlberg's stages. Moral reasoning is set within a larger context of the self's relatedness to an overarching "whole"—a transcendent source of meaning, value, and power. In short, moral reasoning and religious faith are seen as integral parts of the quest for meaning. In Tessa's case, I wanted to understand how interpersonal virtues and vices fit together with the hard paradoxes of faith, specifically the paradoxes of suffering and redemption, sin and salvation. In this case, the dynamics of moral reasoning fit Fowler's description of Stage Three "synthetic-conventional faith."

Fowler refuses to subsume religious faith to moral reasoning. His approach is more neo-Hegelian in that he focuses more on the evolutionary or diachronic transformation of the self-transcendent relationship. At the same time, the requirements of empirical validation make it necessary that he adhere to the principles of structural-developmental psychology. This tension between neo-Kantian constructivism and neo-Hegelian phenomenology of religion persists throughout the theory of faith development.

To the Kantian and Hegelian elements, I would add American pragmatism. The pragmatist conception of belief as an instrumental principle for sorting out experience is transposed into the notion of faith as an instrumental principle of meaning-making, albeit a particular kind of meaning-making, by which we apprehend our relatedness to a transcendent source or sources of meaning and value. From this eclectic mix of epistemologies has come a complex theory which purports to describe the evolution of moral and religious meaning.

In presenting faith development theory to groups throughout North America, it was not unusual to be approached by persons who either wanted to expedite their journey of faith or protested that they were already at the highest stage. North Americans idolize progress and success. Any theory that has the slightest hint of accelerating progress to endpoints where only the elite are to be found is bound to attract popular attention. It is a misperception, however, to assume that faith development has anything to do with expediting any form of human development. Admittedly, the term "faith development" conjures up crude images of persons being energized by "faith" as if they were batteries. Similarly, the concept of a stage loses its historical denotation in Christian spirituality as a resting place along with pilgrimage of faith. Instead, it is viewed as a rung in a ladder of private religiosity to be grasped with deliberate speed and then expeditiously bypassed to meet the next challenge. In these stereotypical images of faith development, there is no room for paradox and no appreciation of the pain of those who struggle to make some sense of their lives in a world fragmented by all kinds of oppression.

I am particularly concerned about the linking of faith and development. As a product of the African diaspora, I am suspicious of developmental models that relegate the experiences of so-called Third World persons to the lowest levels of human development. The idea that faith has anything to do with progress is an anathema to those who suffer in the bowels of personal or social oppression. However, if the goals of development truly reflect the hard paradoxes of faith, then it is appropriate to speak of faith development. In the following discussion of faith development, how the theory reflects the hard paradoxes of faith are of utmost importance.

FAITH AND MEANING-MAKING

Faith is what faith does. It renders meaning and value to the self. Each stage of faith is a novel form of meaning-making. In keeping with its pragmatist connections, valuation is understood as a relational process. The self is formed in a triadic relationship of self, other selves, and a transcendent center or centers of meaning and value.

The term "center of value" is taken from the theology and ethics of H. Richard Niebuhr.[3] It is Niebuhr's way of reformulating Josiah Royce's concept of "loyalty to cause" as an absolute moral principle by which value is constituted. Unlike Royce, Niebuhr is not an idealist. The self owes loyalty not to the principle of loyalty but to the "God beyond the many"—the one God who is the source of loyalty and who calls persons into a covenantal relationship. This theological anthropology is foundational to faith development theory.

Fowler recognizes that not everyone believes in God and that there are multiple centers of value that demand our loyalty, not all of which are religious. Nevertheless, radical monotheism is the normative theological principle governing Fowler's interpretation of the formation of the self. The self is constituted triadically in relation to other selves and to a transcendent God.

Succinctly put, the idea of faith development is intended to capture how we fit together the various parts of the self-other and self-transcendent relationship into a coherent whole. This process is termed the "structuring of meaning." That this activity is termed "faith development" is the subject of considerable debate. If faith is indeed a process of composing parts into a coherent relation to an overarching whole, then considerable attention needs to be paid to the historical contexts, traditions, myths, rituals, and symbols—in short, the contents of faith. More will be said on the structure-content problem. It is sufficient to say here that there is an inherent conflict in faith development theory between the effort to demythologize faith using Piagetian structuralism and to remythologize it using Niebuhrian theological anthropology.

I should add that the demythologizing process is also aided by Wilfred Cantwell Smith's differentiation of religion, faith, and belief. Smith defines religion as a "cumulative tradition"—a product of historical images and symbols, a behavior by which faith is transmitted from generation to generation, from culture to culture.[4] In a later work, he traces the etymological roots of the terms *faith* and *belief*.[5] He argues that both terms have lost their original sense as conveying a unique human propensity to surrender to a transcendent source of meaning and power. From the Latin *credere*, to believe (a hybrid of *cor*, the heart, and *dare*, to give), the English-speaking world has understood belief as a giving of the heart to another. The same applies to cognate terms such as the German *Glaube* (from *lieben*, to love). Smith's extrication of faith from a necessarily religious world view is particularly pertinent to Fowler's appropriation of the structuralist distinction between *structure* and *content*. As a process of meaning-making, faith is described in terms of psychological structures that underlie the ideational content of religious beliefs and behavior.

Religion serves as a historical matrix for the concrete, poetic, and imagistic language of faith. To attempt to separate faith from this matrix in order to comply with the canons of structural-developmental psychology is nothing short of psychological abortion. Having delineated the domain of faith as the structuring of meaning, Fowler realizes that faith cannot be defined exclusively in terms of the transformation of cognitive-affective structures. Hence, he draws attention to "the structuring power of the contents of faith."[6] This only obfuscates the matter. Now we do not really know which structuring activity is in control of faith development. An examination of the stages of development leaves no doubt that the stages coinciding with Piaget's cognitive stages are oriented toward the structuralist end of the paradigm whereas those describing adulthood tilt in favor of the "contents" of faith.

While faith development theory derives little from Smith's project to retrieve the etymological roots of the term *faith*, it owes its conceptual vigor to the theocentrism of H. Richard Niebuhr. Niebuhr, in response to Barth's transcendental faith, characterizes faith as a form of human meaning-making and valuation. So defined, faith is relevant to the interpretation of experience, specifically the experience of the human community as it is formed and transformed in the image of the one God. Fowler agrees with Niebuhr's trinitarian interpretation of God's unfolding character. God is Creator, manifested as power; God is sovereign Governor and Judge, manifested as order; God is Redeemer, manifested as mercy and goodness. These attributes are not idealistic; they have powerful implications for Niebuhr's ethic of responsibility.

According to Niebuhr, the moral self is the responsible self. The moral community is the community that understands itself as a people called into a covenantal relationship with God and with one another. No group, race, or religion has exclusive claim to this relationship. A moral community that is grounded in a radically monotheistic faith and a covenantal ethic of responsibility is prepared to risk losing its particularity in order to respond to the need for including those on the outside.

PRAGMATISM AND FAITH DEVELOPMENT

The sociality of the self and its relation to an overarching "whole" discloses the strong similarity between faith development theory and pragmatism.

Josiah Royce's "pragmatic idealism" gave rise to a theory of the self as a *socius*—a system of social relations that undergoes transformation as it interacts with novel situations while at the same time preserving continuity. The relationship between

43

continuity (the continuous emergence of one system from another) and discontinuity (the appearance of novelty) is reflected in the two constitutive elements of the self, namely, the "I" and the "me." The "me" is the empirical self that is constituted through social interaction. The "me" is made conscious through role-taking. Since the social order revolves from the simple to multiple systems of social interaction, the "me" may be discerned from a number of perspectives. Mead referred to the nexus of organized social relations as the "generalized other."[7]

The "I" functions as the center of awareness, the seat of spontaneity and creativity that is known only through its objectification in the "me"—in other words, through the thoughts and actions of others. Mead places the burden of self-consciousness on social interaction. Language, including the gestures of childhood, is the medium of communication. However, he does not intend to portray the individual as a chameleon or a puppet. Rather, he is trying to accommodate the dynamics of change and constancy in the development of the self. In this effort, he coins the term "sociality" to denote the accommodation of past and present or old and new systems of interaction.

The mark of sociality is the changing self as it responds to multiple perspectives. But even in the midst of change, the self preserves its unity. As in William James, the integrated self endures the changing flux of experience. James, Dewey, and Mead try to preserve the empirical validity of the self as the latter is known through social interaction. At the same time, they do not want a self that is wholly determined by social interaction. Herein lies a dilemma for pragmatism. Determinism, including behaviorism and divine omnipotence, is an anathema. At the same time, the pragmatists acknowledge that the moral imperative to change self and world does not result in the triumph of good over evil. James therefore speculates on a finite God—one who depends on the human for assistance in transforming persons and the world. Dewey appeals to "a common faith" for the moral transformation of the world, enhanced and mediated by democracy and education.

As a pragmatic idealist, Mead does not discount metaphysical aspects of the self. Pragmatically, the "I" and the "me" have different functions in the integration of the self. But this functional relationship does not fully explain the unity of the self. There is a metaphysical dimension that is also to be considered. This is realized in the "I"—the transcendent and numenal core of the self. Mead does not ground this transcendence in an *a priori* relation to God. In each of these pragmatists, there is no appeal to divine revelation. Empiricism takes precedence over revelation.

On this point, Niebuhr and the pragmatists part company. Niebuhr is less idealistic than Mead or Fowler in dealing with sin and evil. Mead is utterly optimistic about the ultimate harmony of social interaction. The social process is the environment in which salvation is enacted. Royce's idealist view of loyalty to Cause provides a moral philosophical basis for this optimism. Niebuhr is less sanguine about the human capacity for sin, self-deception, and evil. These are not transcended by the social process but stand in tension with the goodness of God's creation, sovereignty, and redemption. Through faith in God, we find meaning and value in the face of sin and evil.

Fowler joins Kohlberg in linking the concept of decentration to Mead's symbolic interactionist view of the self as a developing complex of relational role-taking activities. Through role-taking the self is transformed. This is the extent of Mead's analysis of social change. Mead took the "I" for granted, anchoring it in the roles played by the social self (the "generalized other"). James, on the other hand, was interested not only in the material, social, and spiritual manifestations of the "me" but also in the volitional and purposeful character of the "I."[8]

Erikson, whose ideas also form part of the backdrop of faith development theory, appropriates some of Mead's social psychology but also leans more favorably toward a recognition of the religious core of identity formation. The "me" is the self that is known in interaction with others. The "I" is both the observing center of awareness and the core of ego-identity whose continuity endures in the midst of changing stages of identity formation. Erikson acknowledges the transcendent core of the "I"—dramatically experienced as the "counter-player" whom Moses encountered on Mt. Sinai, the "I AM that I AM."[9]

The belief that humanity is deeply grounded in relationship to a transcendent center of meaning and value is a seminal feature of faith development theory.

STAGES AND STRUCTURES

A cardinal point in Piaget's theory of cognitive development is its view that knowledge is *constructed* through the interaction of innate cognitive structures and assimilable data from the environment. Assimilation and accommodation denote the dialectical processes of cognitive development. Assimilation refers to the process by which data from the environment are incorporated by available cognitive structures; accommodation is the process by which the internal structures are transformed as data are assimilated from the environment. Cognitive development as a process of adaptation to the environment is defined by the dialectical paradigm of assimilation and accommodation.[10]

The concept of structure is a useful heuristic metaphor for addressing the dialectic of constancy and change. Borrowed from gestalt psychology, a structure is a covert system of transformations that is inferred from the observation of overt patterns of behavior. The key point about cognitive structures is that they comprise elements logically related to one another. On the basis of the concept of structure, it is feasible to chart the progress of the biological organism toward a specific end-state, and the functions or activities by which this goal is achieved. Present and past activities are explained in terms of the future direction of the organism.

The concept of structure is also a historical schema for explaining the various stages by which a pre-existent state was transformed into the present state. Both teleological and historical schemata are present in Piaget's stages, though greater emphasis is placed on the mechanism of historical progression through the transformation of cognitive structures.

Marx Wartofsky suggests that Piaget's theory is "teleonomic" rather than teleological since there is no conscious goal that is being sought by the developing organism.[11]

At this time, it might be helpful to review Piaget's stages of cognitive development. Briefly, these stages are: (1) sensorimotor operations; (2) pre-concrete operations; (3) concrete operations; and (4) formal operations or abstract logical thought.

The first thing to be said about these stages is that they are sequentially ordered. It is logically impossible for the second stage to precede the first, and so on. The emergence of a stage may be prevented, accelerated, or retarded by environmental, psychological, or biological factors, but the sequence remains constant.

A second characteristic of Piaget's stages is that they are hierarchical integrations; that is, the higher stage integrates the structures of the preceding stages into a "structured whole" *(structures d'ensemble)*, which, paradoxically, is qualitatively different from the preceding and following stages. Succeeding stages are not simply added to the preceding ones. Each stage is a qualitative reorganization of the preceding ones into a new configuration of experience. The emphasis on qualitative change implies that earlier behavior continues to exist even though there is a change in the dominant mode. Identifying what is continuing behavior is not as clearcut as identifying transformational change.

A third characteristic of Piaget's stages is their ambiguity. Earlier and current cognitive and affective operations co-exist. Furthermore, the duration of each stage varies. Hence, the concept of stage is not only confusing but also of little usefulness. Even Piaget admits that an individual might have implicit or explicit options to employ different stages of cognition depending on the area of activity with which she or he is involved at a particular time.

A fourth characteristic of Piaget's stages is their claim to universality. That these stages are found in every culture is debatable. Ultimately, the claim of universality rests on the first characteristic already mentioned—their invariable sequence. This assumes that interaction between the self and the environment follows a logical configuration of cognitive processes.

This raises the question of the difference between maturation and development. Piaget limits maturation to biological growth. As far as he is concerned, cognitive development involves biological and environmental factors. Development includes maturation and refers to the unfolding of levels of organization. Maturation without development amounts to "genesis without structuralism." Similarly, development without maturation is "structuralism without genesis."

To summarize, a stage in Piaget's theory refers to the diachronic or historical evolution of synchronic or equilibrated cognitive structures. This unfolding of structures occurs as the individual interacts with the external environment. The environment provides the datum of experience. Hence, constructivists are mainly concerned with how the environment is known and altered through the application of particular individual cognitive and affective structures, and conversely, how the environment affects the transformation of these structures. In other words, the environment is functionally determined by the individual insofar as what is assimilated and accommodated by appropriate structures is considered an environmental stimulus for the construction of knowledge.

With the foregoing information as background to faith development theory, let us look more closely at the trajectory of the stages of faith.

STAGES OF FAITH

Drawing on Piagetian structuralism, Fowler argues that persons are purposively engaged in making meaning of their lives. The progression of the stages of meaning-making is governed by a clearly defined *telos*, namely, a normative covenantal community of persons-in-relation to one another and to the divine. This vision of human relationships emulates the biblical tradition of a people called into a covenant with God. In other words, there is a particular theological anthropology in faith development theory, the principal components of which are vocation and covenant. The human vocation is to recover the basic ontological interconnectedness of the divine and the human. But whereas Fowler limits his ontology to the relationship between the divine and the human, I would extend the ontology of relatedness to include all of creation. We need to image the Creator within a covenantally established created order that also includes the natural environment. In the words of theologian Douglas John Hall, "This silent partner of our covenantal being is no longer willing to remain dumb before its shearers."[12]

In sum, faith development theory operates on a covenantal metaphor. Each stage is an imaging of what persons are called to be in relation to a transcendent center of meaning.

In an earlier work I referred to the concept of structure in faith development theory as "a principle of coherence governing human becoming."[13] My intent then was to expand the metaphor of structure beyond its strictly organic-biological purview. I argued that the vectors of a stage of faith included more activities than those required for a stage in Piaget's theory. I would like now to focus on the dialectic of transition and transformation in stages of faith, and on the role of paradox.

A stage in faith development is a period in the life cycle when these activities are integrated into a "structured whole." The vectors identified by Fowler are: (a) form of logic, (b) social perspective-taking, (c) form of moral judgment, (d) bounds of social awareness, (e) locus of authority, (f) form of world coherence, and (g) symbolic functioning. Without going into the developmental trajectory of each vector, let me give an overview of the stages and the process of transition from one to another.

A Pre-stage: Primal or Undifferentiated Faith

This stage presumes the existence of a trustworthy ethos for the emerging infant. It affirms the presence of the numinous in the relationship between mother and child. In this primal state of undifferentiated otherness, the burden rests on the primary caregiver to transmit a sense of wholeness that flows from a basic ontology of communion between the divine and the human.

TRANSITION   The psychological explanation for transition from this stage is the onset of differentiation and integration. Cognitively and affectively, the child is able to perceive otherness that is separate from self by decentering and disembedding from the primal state of equilibrium.

Stage One: Intuitive-Projective Faith

This stage is linked directly to biological maturation, specifically, the formation of egocentric thought and the acquisition of language. According to Piagetian cognition, the child (usually around six years old) is pre-operational; that is, she or he is unable to distinguish concrete reality from fantasy. Consequently, meaning-making is fantasy-filled, thinking is episodic and one-dimensional. In short, dependence on the imagination is paramount as the child responds to a multiplicity of stimuli from the immediate environment.

TRANSITION   Transition to stage two (usually in the seventh year) is brought about by the development of concrete operational thought. Accordingly, transition is characterized by a mixture of pre-operational and operational thinking.

Stage Two: Mythic-Literal Faith

In this stage the ability to order the world in meaningful patterns and to classify objects through concepts of causality, space, and time is coupled with a fascination for narrative and story. The latter are comprehended literally as the child relies on her own logic and projects herself into the fabric of the narrative. Play is enacted narrative. The nexus of interpersonal relations is widened beyond the immediate parental and familial environment to include peers and other authority figures.

TRANSITION   Transition to stage three (usually in adolescence around age twelve) is marked by the development of mutual perspective-taking; that is, the child is now able to construct the interiority of the other and to see himself as he is seen by others, hence the concern for the status of interpersonal relationships. In terms of Piaget's stages of cognitive development, this process requires the onset of formal operations.

Stage Three: Synthetic-Conventional Faith

The center of value in this stage is interpersonal harmony, loyalty, and trustworthiness. There is a strong inclination to resolve contradictions and conflict by locating them in the external world or by appealing to shared feelings and traditionally approved interpersonal virtues. The self that is constituted is a synthesis of perspectives, values, and feelings held by "significant others." A conventionally acknowledged "generalized other," such as school or church, is tacitly maintained as the self's ultimate point of reference.

TRANSITION Transition to stage four is complex. Stage three is the norm of subjects interviewed in the United States. Accordingly, there are adult as well as adolescent examples of stage four.

What then are the criteria of stage transition? Evidently, certain aspects of American culture nurture a protracted stage-three construction of meaning. Formal operations or abstract logical thinking is present, but the self remains embedded in its matrix of social relations and conventionally held interpersonal virtues. The presence of adults at stage three sharpens the distinction between maturation and development. Biologically speaking, these persons have matured, but there is no continuing development of new structures of meaning-making. At the same time, we find adolescents who are still in process of biological maturation but who also exhibit characteristics identical to those of stage-three adults. The co-existence of adolescent and adult cases of stage three suggests that stage three marks the limit of usefulness of the Piagetian paradigm of cognitive-structural development.

Consistency with the earlier criteria of stage transition would require a stage beyond formal operations. But this is not the case. Holding to the Piagetian paradigm has required that the stage of formal operations be divided into an early phase (stage three) and a late phase (stage four). The basic difference is in the *function* of formal operations. At stage three, the onset of formal

51

operations is readily observable. Evidently, a particular kind of relationship between person and environment is required for transition to stage four, namely, one that provides radical cognitive and affective discontinuity with the conventional social milieu. In other words, it is the experience of conflict and contradiction in the relationship between the changing individual and the changing world that leads to stage transition.

In the *Manual for Faith Development Research,* we assumed that this relationship presupposes the maturation of formal operational thinking.[14] In retrospect, we should have paid more attention to the dialectical relationship between the changing individual and the changing world. There is no doubt that transition to stage four revolves around the ability of the individual to take on the contradictions and conflicts between self and world. This requires disembedding from the primary reference group in which the self is defined.

Stage Four: Individuative-Reflective Faith

This stage is marked by a decisive distancing from conventionally acknowledged sources of authority and by a concerted effort to evaluate the truth claims of ideological systems. The concern for the logical justification of world views and faith commitments is made possible by fully developed formal operational logic. The emergence of an autonomous self is coupled with a need to define the self in terms of personally selected ideas and values. This disembedding of the self from traditionally derived relationships may also be accompanied by a sense of commitment to self-chosen rules for governing relationships. Ideological imperialism and fanaticism are real possibilities at this stage.

TRANSITION   The impact of social and historical influences at stage four suggests that this stage may reflect peculiar features of American culture, for example the movement of young adults away from the familial niche to the college campus, and the onset of a "psychosocial moratorium."[15] Consequently, stage four may be a protracted period of psychological maturation, lasting for several years.

If conflict or disequilibrium is the agent of stage transition, how is it indicated at this stage? The autonomous self established at stage four is now vulnerable to a plurality of conflict-producing experiences, for example, vocational and intergenerational conflict. An important developmental task is to make sense of the multiple constituencies that demand loyalty and commitment. The tendency at this stage is to dichotomize the world into isolated and absolute options for the resolution of conflict. This precludes any possibility of further transformation. Stage transition occurs only when the individual is able to integrate the dialectical tensions of living in a culturally pluralistic world where the composing of meaning involves competing reference groups and centers of value. The integration of opposites is appropriately represented by the metaphor of conjunctive faith.

Stage Five: Conjunctive Faith

Multiple social perspective-taking is the central activity operating in this stage. Multiple perspectives are held in tension in the interest of discovering a more inclusive truth that transcends the partial claims of any one perspective. This multi-perspectival approach to reality heightens the role of language, particularly metaphor and symbol, as a medium of human understanding. Only metaphor is capable of communicating the tentativeness of human understanding. Similarly, symbols alone hold in tension irreconcilable opposites. Of particular significance is the hermeneutic of dialogue as a process for reaching consensus on the meaning and truth disclosed in religious classics. Persons at this stage submit themselves to what David Tracy calls a "journey of intensification" into the "liberating paradox" of the particularity of their traditions and their claims of universality.[16]

The introduction of paradox at stage five is rather late. This is the result of being too wedded to the Piagetian paradigm. Paradox is accorded the status of an advanced level of cognitive functioning, namely, the "ironic imagination."[17] The emergence of paradoxical knowing is a necessary step for transition to the final stage.

Transition to Stage Six: Universalizing Faith

This final stage of faith concretely demonstrates the content-structure problem in faith development theory. Here, structure as the term is understood in Piagetian structuralism has exhausted its usefulness. For one thing, the empirical validity of stage six is yet to be verified by longitudinal studies. Persons whom Fowler regards as exemplars of this stage, such as Martin Luther King, Jr., the Mahatma Gandhi, and Mother Teresa of Calcutta, are undoubtedly worthy of acclaim for their moral and religious commitments, but they were not subjected to the standard research procedures for identifying a stage of faith. Whether one has to be among the elite transformers of social justice to qualify for stage six remains to be seen.

The pivotal feature of this stage is the complex of philosophical, theological, and ethical principles that it represents. Stage six describes an ontology of communion or universal "commonwealth of being." According to Fowler, the logic demonstrated by persons at this stage is "synthetic" in contrast to the "dialectical" logic of stage five. This distinction is highly speculative. "Synthetic logic" refers to the capacity to hold opposites in tension. It is a both-and paradox—a *coincidentia oppositorum*. The philosophical idea behind this concept is a neo-Hegelian evolution of a uniting Spirit *(Geist)* that binds humanity in an overarching "Whole." That this is embodied in particular individuals is the most crucial claim of stage six.

In spite of its Hegelian overtones, this final stage reflects H. Richard Niebuhr's covenantal ethic of responsibility and radical monotheism. "Universalizing faith" is a portrait of the person as reconciler of human community, one whose multi-perspectival consciousness of "synthetic logic" allows him or her to vivify the unity underlying the fragmentation of the world. This stage involves an ethical commitment to solidarity with victims and faith born of love, both of which few of us mortals can claim as the truth of our lives. Clearly, it has to be admitted that this portrait of the person goes far beyond the empirical limitations of Piagetian cognitive developmental psychology. This final stage calls into question the limitations of cognitive developmental psychology for interpreting the paradoxical and symbolic dimensions of faith.

METAPHOR AND PARADOX

At the outset I should note that Fowler has sought to change the conventional grammatical usage of the term "faith" from a noun to a verb and to extricate faith from its conventional religious habitus. In addition, he suggests that the term "logic" in faith development theory be understood metaphorically.[18] In this concluding section, I would like to expand on a metaphorical interpretation of faith development.

According to Sallie McFague,

> A metaphor is a word or phrase used *in*appropriately. It belongs properly in one context but is being used in another. . . . It is an attempt to say something about the unfamiliar in terms of the familiar, an attempt to speak about what we do not know in terms of what we do know. . . . Metaphor always has the character of "is" and "is not": an assertion is made but as a likely account rather than a definition.[19]

McFague notes that not all metaphors fit this definition because of their embeddedness in conventional language. She recommends that "fresh" metaphors are necessary for conducting theology in an ecological, nuclear age.

I suggest that this is precisely what Fowler intends by the term "faith development." The problem is that we have not one but two fresh metaphors and they do not always work in tandem; in fact, they oppose each other in some critical ways. This opposition stems from the eclectic mixture of developmental psychology, pragmatic philosophy, and theology. Each of these disciplines has its peculiar understanding of metaphor. For example, the requirements for normativity demanded by developmental psychology go against the tentativeness (and perhaps humility) of metaphorical theology. As far as the latter is concerned, what is being expressed indirectly cannot be expressed directly. Kierkegaard's maieutic art (indirect communication) is a paradigm of metaphorical theology. Through metaphor we are able to accommodate paradox—either-or and both-and.[20]

McFague sets forth three fundamental characteristics of theology.

> The first thing to say is that theology, as constructive and metaphorical, does not "demythologize" but "remythologizes." To envision theology as metaphorical means, at the outset, to refute the attempt to denude religious language of its concrete, poetic, imagistic, and hence inevitably anthropomorphic, character, in the search for presumably more enlightened (and usually more abstract) terminology. It is to accept as one of theology's primary tasks remythologizing for our time: identifying and elucidating primary metaphors and models from contemporary experience which will express Christian faith in powerful, illuminating ways.[21]

I have already expressed my views on the demythologizing aspects of faith development theory. The theory is also an opportunity for remythologizing religious faith by illumining its mythic and symbolic dimensions.

The second feature of theology according to McFague is that it is metaphorical. There is something incomplete about metaphors. They are and are not yet. This metaphoric tension pushes against closed structural stages.

The third characteristic of theology identified by McFague is that it is heuristic.

> A metaphorical theology is necessarily a heuristic venture: it insists that new metaphors and models be given a chance, be tried out as likely accounts of the God-world relationship, be allowed to make a case for themselves.[22]

Without a metaphorical theology, faith development theory is easily reduced to the empiricism of cognitive developmental psychology or to theological and philosophical idealism. At stake is the definition of faith as "the structuring of meaning." Recognizing the potential for empiricist reductionism, Fowler proposes that faith be understood as an activity of the imagination.[23] This is terribly important, for it heightens the functions of metaphor, symbol, paradox, and narrative in faith development theory. In examining these elements, it becomes clear that a salient feature of metaphor is that it functions analogically.[24] This is crucial to faith development theory. We could say that its logic is "ana-logic." In other words, the coherence or integration of the self exemplified by a stage of faith is analogous to what the relationship to the transcendent is like.

In terms of cognitive developmental psychology, a stage of faith is a configuration of meaning-making functions. But, understood metaphorically, a stage of faith is a paradigm of the self-transcendent relationship at a particular time in the narrative history of the self. Here, I am adopting Garrett Green's definition of a paradigm as,

> an exemplar or ideal type—because it shows forth a pattern, a coherent nexus of relations, in a simple and straightforward manner. Paradigms function heuristically by revealing the constitutive patterns in more complex aspects of our experience that might otherwise remain recalcitrant, incoherent, or bewildering.[25]

A metaphorical reading of the stages helps us to see their heuristic function and to preserve the tension between religious and scientific paradigms in faith development theory. Moreover, the theory makes intelligible the imaginative and mysterious function of faith in confirming our relation to the transcendent.

To summarize this chapter, developmental stage theories explicitly or implicitly articulate an ethical theory of what persons ought to become. Fowler's theory of faith development articulates a normative portrait of not only mature faith but also how such faith develops. A significant problem in the theory is its fusion or confusion of empiricism and idealism. This is especially evident in the final stage. In recommending a metaphorical interpretation of logic, Fowler implies that neither constructivist empiricism nor neo-Hegelian idealism can adequately account for the actual practice of faith and its expression through religious language. I agree with Janet Martin Soskice that "empiricist or idealist analyses of model and metaphor in religious language are only really attractive if it is judged that realism has failed."[26] But clearly there are realist presuppositions in faith development theory, chief among which is the claim that it is conceptually possible to depict the self-transcendent relationship without having to prove the existence of the transcendent. This is accomplished by means of metaphor. To paraphrase Soskice, the realist position is that theory is informed by the world even though it may never adequately describe the world. Faith development theory is faced with the problem of specifying the experiences and particular communities of moral and religious discourse that inform its understanding of faith. In so doing, essential experiences that are omitted should also be acknowledged. For example, we need to question whether the hard paradoxes of existence are glossed over in the desire to chart the process by which a coherent structure of meaning and value is established in relation to a transcendent center of meaning and power.

Fowler has attempted to do what is intended by metaphorical theology, namely—to express in a novel and unconventional way the relationship between persons, God, and the world. This he has done by forging new links between theology and the social sciences. In the following chapter, we will see how dialectical psychology, operating out of an appreciation of the elusive, contrary, and paradoxical contours of human existence, complements metaphorical theology in interpreting the changing relationship between a changing self and a changing world.

CHAPTER THREE

DIALECTICAL
TRANSFORMATIONS

The limited role prescribed by Piaget for the environment has drawn serious criticism from social scientists who are concerned about the interdependence of the changing person and the changing socio-historical world.[1] Dialectical psychologists hold that dialectical conflict is a fundamental characteristic of cognition and creativity that continues throughout life history. This dialectic is not limited to the compensatory relationship between assimilation and accommodation in Piaget's cognitive developmental psychology but extends over the full range of social interaction. The relationship between the changing individual and the changing historical-cultural situation perpetuates a structure of social interaction in which knowledge is constructed. This continuing task of living with dialectical conflicts and contradictions defines human development.

In short, dialectical psychologists maintain a broad ecological view of human development. They take into consideration the multiple circumstances within which persons interact, the multidimensionality of experience, and the multiple reference groups to which the self responds throughout the life span.

Dialectical psychologists therefore adopt an interdisciplinary life-span approach to human development. Their objective is to expand the concept of development beyond its strictly biological (organismic) roots as a process of *adaptation* to the environment, and to emphasize *constant change* over adaptation.

This emphasis on the human ability to effect change brings

into sharper focus two aspects of development. First is the fact that persons, interacting with their changing environment, are producers as well as products of their development. Second, any change must be viewed in the light of other changes with which it is dialectically related. For example, the relation between the changing structures of meaning-making and the changing self.

In this chapter, I intend to make a case for the dialectical transformation of self and world.

THE SELF AND MEANING-MAKING

John Broughton maintains that in structural-developmental psychology, "the whole concept of ontogeny is premised upon the possibility of the removal of egocentricity."[2] This continuing process of disembedding from previous ways of constructing meaning is the key to Robert Kegan's theory of the transformation of the self. Kegan combines psychoanalytic theory of *internalization* and Piagetian cognitive-developmental theory of *decentration* to interpret the decentering or disembedding of the self from egocentrism. Both internalization and decentration refer to the overcoming of egocentrism in the self-other relationship. Once the developing self is able to differentiate self from other, then what was externalized can be internalized. Similarly, decentration involves the development of the ability to differentiate between subject and object. Its development is marked by increasingly complex forms of social perspective-taking.

Two factors must be underscored. First, the self is formed as it interacts with the world. Second, there are stages of relative stability as the self progresses from egocentrism to higher levels of social perspective-taking. In the course of development, the self is liberated from its captivity in the egocentric perceptions of early childhood.[3] Kegan, however, does not use the term "faith" to characterize the construction of meaning. Nor does he speculate on the self's relation to a transcendent source of meaning. The construction of meaning depends on the ability of the self to overcome dualisms of subject and object, self and world, and so on, by dialectically differentiating and integrating them into a coherent system of meaning. In short, Kegan

upholds the continuing transformation of the self as it disembeds
from previous constructions of its relation to the world.

Fowler is also concerned with the problem of the continuing
transformation of the self-world relationship, but he sets this
relationship within the wider self-transcendent relationship.
This latter relationship provides the basis for "faith knowing"
and "moral knowing."

> *In both faith-knowing and the kind of moral-knowing which gives rise to
> choice and action, the constitution and modification of the self is always
> an issue.* In these kinds of constitutive-knowing not only is the
> "known" being constructed but there is also a simultaneous
> confirmation, modification, or reconstruction of the *knower in
> relation to the known.*[4]

This statement implies that Fowler does not consider the self's
relationship to the physical world an arena in which dialectical
transformation occurs. Nevertheless, I think his intent is to argue
that constructivist psychology fails to explain the dialectical
transformation of the self-world relationship. But Fowler does
not make a clean break with constructivism. He still wants to
satisfy the constructivist demands for equilibrated stages. This
only contributes to the fragmentation of reality into different
spheres of action, each with its unique form of cognition.

The dialectical approach not only focuses on particular
spheres of activity in which the value of the self is at stake but
also widens the horizons of the self's interaction with the world.
This has particular implications for religious conversion.

LATERAL AND STRUCTURAL CONVERSION

All too often, testimonies of religious conversion are limited
to a dramatic transformation in one arena of life history, usually
the moral. We can easily point to changes in moral behavior.
"What I used to do, I do no longer," or the more popular
expression, "I became saved" at some noteworthy time and
place. It is much more difficult to hold these in balance with
other critical arenas of life. An example is the seminarian who,
having professed a "born again" experience, later discovers that

the "born again" experience has to be brought into conversation with other experiences, which impinge on her or his understanding of being called by God to the ordained ministry.

My point is that the contours of transformation should not be defined by one particular experience. Other experiences may very well negate the claims of transformation. Not every vector of life follows the same progression. Declarations of change in one area of life may very well be the result of conflicts in other areas. It is no wonder then that testimonies of religious conversion are often accompanied by extreme fanaticism as converts try to defend their conversion from the intrusion of other arenas of life.

Dialectical psychology describes the course of development as open-ended. It is not charted as a sequence of structural stages. What we regard as a stage or "structured whole" may be a defensive posture against conflict and contradiction. Instead of structural stages, therefore, we have synchrony between different progressions, some of which may be in conflict with one another. Synchrony refers to a tentative confluence of historical forces in the self-world relationship that leads to a reconfiguring of the self-world relationship. What brings about the reconfiguring or rebalancing of the self-world relationship is an intentional effort to bring this tentative equilibrium into dialogue with what is left out in the balancing act. In short, synchrony calls for a hermeneutic of suspicion. We have to ask then what is being left out in the experience of equilibrium, continuity, and coherence.

In an earlier study, I proposed a typology of religious conversion based on the theory of faith development.[5] I suggested that the content-structure dualism in a structural-developmental interpretation of religious conversion resulted in two types of conversion—*lateral* and *structural*. I defined lateral conversion as a change in ideational content as indicated by the change in religious affiliation or commitment. My research was conducted during a period of religious awakening in this country when thousands of Americans were infatuated with exotic gurus, swamis, and other pundits from the Orient. Americans were converting from one group to another as new and improved formulae for spiritual enlightenment came on the market. Utilitarian individualism was rampant in the conversion marketplace. My interviews with converts who moved from group to group indicated that this movement did not involve stage change. I referred to this type of change as *lateral conversion.*

In contrast, I applied the term *structural conversion* to persons who underwent a change in stage in their conversion or conversions. The distinction between these two types of conversion was based on a bold attempt to do empirical research on faith development theory. My analysis was rather speculative, given the rudimentary status of the theory and the uncertainty of its empirical validity.[6]

Since I did not conduct longitudinal studies of my subjects, the identification of a stage of faith development was based entirely on their retrospective narratives. Structural conversion, precipitated by a conversion experience, followed logically from the criteria established for movement from one stage to another. Fowler and others have adopted this typology of lateral and structural conversions.[7]

In retrospect, I should have been more cognizant of dialectical transformations. In studying religious converts, I tried to discover how elements were integrated into a pattern of relations. The integrated self was my root metaphor. At stage three, the integrated self revolved around belonging to the group. The religious affections, harmony, and the magnetism of affiliating with significant others were definitive of this stage. I found subjects whose conversion from one group to another was fueled by powerful bonds of affection.

Here a case history is illustrative.

THE CASE OF VICTOR

Victor is a brilliant young man, a student at a prestigious Ivy League university, the son of a prominent educator and public servant. His family moved up the ladder of university presidencies and affiliated with religious denominations that reflected their social status. At the time of the interview, they were Episcopalians.

Victor grew up with a strong sense of God as his personal friend who gave him his first girlfriend, was his constant companion, got him selected to the basketball team, and protected him from bullies in high school. He remarked that God was always on the other end of the telephone. In adolescence Victor made the rounds of churches with his parents, eventually attending a prominent Episcopal church in his hometown.

Soon after enrolling in college, Victor met some friends in his evangelical fellowship and started attending their church. He was attracted to the warmth of the relationships, the simplicity of the services, the simplicity of the rituals, the harmonious accord on all matters of belief. Not long afterward, Victor met a proselyte of another religious group, which resided together in a commune. He was enamored with their affection, their messianic and apocalyptic prophecies, and literal reading of the Bible. The leader of this group called himself Jesus Christ and his wife was affectionately known as the Holy Spirit. Victor had found himself another home away from home. It was only natural that he would try to bring his parents into this fellowship. But before doing so, he had to resolve conflicts regarding the different interpretations of Scripture upheld by the evangelical fellowship and the Jesus commune. Accordingly, Victor arranged a debate between these two groups.

As the debate proceeded, it became evident that the members of the evangelical fellowship were becoming more and more angry with the Jesus folks. Victor could not resolve the differences in their truth claims. The deciding factor for him was the intolerance and hostility of the evangelical fellowship. And so off to the Jesus commune he went. His conversion was ensured and conflict pushed aside.

Like Job's friends, Victor's friends confronted him with questions. They assaulted his intelligence and insisted that he check out his religious conversion with the college chaplain and a psychiatrist. This threw Victor into a state of apocalyptic confusion. In desperation he checked out the definition of the term "agnostic" in his dictionary, got down on his knees, and asked God to forgive him for declaring himself an agnostic.

I viewed Victor's conversion to the Jesus group as a lateral conversion from the evangelical fellowship. The dynamics of stage three were apparent. Guided by the metaphor of the "integrated self," I looked for stability, coherence, and resolution of conflict. These were clearly evident. Also evident were signs of the "individuated self"—one at odds with the traditional ordering of reality. I concluded that Victor's declaration of agnosticism was indicative of the beginning of transition to stage four, "individuative-reflective faith."

It is very easy to see religious conversion as the resolution of conflict—moral, emotional, or spiritual. The metaphor of the paradoxical self goes against such victory. It signals that transformation is unfinished. The center of gravity is not the resolution of conflict but the paradox—the paradox of struggle and surrender, fulfillment and emptiness, *plerosis* and *kenosis*.

The moral imperative is to move beyond where we are, not necessarily to a higher stage of moral reasoning in which *is* and *ought* are integrated, or to a higher stage of meaning-making in which the cognitive and affective cohere as a structured whole. Rather, it is to move more purposefully and vigorously into the struggle between is and ought, between the selves that we are and the selves that we ought to be. Kierkegaard sums it up nicely as becoming a self before God.[8] Here the recognition that the self is grounded in an infinite relationship to God casts doubt on our efforts to make the elements of finite existence fit together into a coherence stage of meaning, for the self is pricked by the realization that nothing short of existing in relation to God is acceptable—God is "always in the right" and the self is "always in the wrong."[9] In the struggle to live with this paradox, Victor proclaimed himself an agnostic.

A DIALECTICAL-PARADOXICAL HERMENEUTIC

The *telos* of faith development is awesome. Given the psychological requirements for an integrated self, the moral imperatives of covenantal ethics, the "redemptive subversiveness" and self-sacrificial demands of social justice, and the goal of preserving the unity and wholeness of the creation, we need to ask whether any normal human being can fully exemplify "universalizing faith." In the absence of longitudinal studies, we can only hope that such persons would enhance the universe. It would be foolish to pin our hopes for the moral and religious transformation of the world on representatives of the final stage of faith development. Faced with the absence of concrete manifestations of stage-six "principled morality," Kohlberg conflated stages five and six. In the absence of longitudinal data on persons at stage six, Fowler might have to do the same. The key issue is the preeminence of empiricism over hermeneutics, specifically, a closed system of stages over open-ended transformations.

In an early version of the theory of faith development, one of the vectors of a stage of faith was "critical issues with which faith must deal." These issues included suffering and tragedy. This was in recognition of the negative dialectic that pushes against the structuring of meaning. In other words, implicit in the definition of faith as meaning-making is the negation of meaninglessness. Meaninglessness, tragedy, and suffering were regarded as "content" issues that could not be staged. Though critical to faith development theory, these issues continue to be enigmatic for its structuralist hermeneutic.

Fowler's "logic of conviction" is intended as an alternative mode of cognition for apprehending the nonstructural dimensions of meaning-making. This means that practically everything in the domain of faith is "known" primarily by a "logic of conviction." This is even more apparent in adulthood when issues of suffering and meaninglessness loom high in daily life. In this case, the "logic of rational certainty" is of little significance. It is necessary but not sufficient.

Two hermeneutical strategies at work in the same theory is confusing, especially when there is lack of clarity about their relation to each other. The "logic of rational certainty" echoes Kant's philosophy of practical reason. This logic is a necessary condition of human experience. It defines a particular way of relating to the world. But Fowler, unlike Kant, does not limit faith to the human mind. The "logic of conviction" is intended to broaden the relation to the world beyond the rational ordering of experience. By maintaining the complementarity of the two forms of logic, Fowler avoids a serious methodological problem raised by the relation between Piagetian genetic psychology and genetic epistemology, namely, the logical priority of empirical questions about the process of cognition over conceptual questions about the nature of knowledge. The "logic of conviction" is a way of acknowledging that conceptual questions about the nature of faith are not answered by the "logic of rational certainty." However, the dominance of the structuralist paradigm in faith development suggests that the "logic of rational certainty" is logically prior to convictional knowing.

The relationship between these two forms of logic, if it is at all appropriate to consider convictional knowing a form of logic, needs further clarification. Faith is not entirely an empirical phenomenon whose normativity rests on observable patterns or stages. Nor is it entirely a vague epistemic concept that is free of empirical study. To say that faith is both is to acknowledge at the outset that we must find some middle ground for addressing the empirical and conceptual issues. Short of relying on common religious usage of the term "faith," any joint empirical, developmental, and analytical philosophical investigation of faith will require some middle ground for bridging the gap between these two disciplines.

The point of departure for a contextual-dialectical hermeneutic is the changing self and its historical basis of self-understanding. Here I draw on Toulmin's argument that a primary issue for developmental psychologists is "the *changing* relationship between linguistic, linguamorphic, and language-independent elements in cognition."[10] Thus, "If we wish to identify definite and distinct 'stages' in psychological development, that changing relationship promises to be one of the key variables."[11]

In short, we need to focus on the dialectic of constancy and change. Faith development relies heavily on constant patterns of linguistic behavior and, in true Piagetian structuralist fashion, assumes that its interactionist epistemology adequately accounts for the role played by the environment or socialization. I suspect that the concept of convictional knowing is an attempt to attend to the nonlinguistically ordered and nonsequential dimensions of faith such as the imagination, the changing world, and meaninglessness, all of which may present discontinuities that negate the orderly and unambiguous sequence of stages.

It would make sense therefore to minimize the significance of stages. On this point I am entirely in agreement with Toulmin's comment that we should regard the notion of stages simply as "a descriptive convenience rather than a matter of great theoretical significance; and, the more levels we embrace in a single sequence of 'stages,' the vaguer and more arbitrary our subdivision will become."[12] The objective is to avoid the trap of specifying a law of development based upon a single succession of stages. According to Toulmin, development is epigenetic rather than genetic in that it involves a constellation of activities—linguistic, nonlinguistic, symbolic, behavioral, and so on, which fit together in different patterns and evolve at different points in the life of the individual. This is the intent of the "aspects" of faith development.

The problem is that a stage of faith is computed on the basis of averaging the "structural" features of the responses to specific questions that coincide with the aspects. Variations and discontinuities in the aspects are ignored or explained as evidence of stage transition. The fact that aspects are usually out of step with one another—hence, that numerical averaging is necessary—should raise serious questions about the normativity of stages. A dialectical hermeneutic is intended to emphasize the fact that whatever is identified as a constellation of meaning is merely a mixture of continuities and discontinuities, constancy and change. Faith is always more than its empirical stages. This "more than" quality, the "surplus of meaning," has to do with the paradox of seeking the eternal in the temporal. Whatever is identified as a stage is and is not yet. If there is any normativity to stages of faith, it is this paradoxical quality. This "is and is not yet" quality takes us into the realm of theology and ethics. Thus, Toulmin suggests that in developmental psychology, the conception of "maturity" inevitably commits us to "an ethical opinion about the 'true nature' of Man."[13]

Fowler alludes to the theological and ethical dimension of mature faith by framing the final stage in terms of the paradox of *telos* and *eschaton*. Here the necessity of temporal stages is juxtaposed against the mysterious and eternal possibilities of transformation that are effected by the God beyond all gods.

A dialectical-paradoxical hermeneutic of faith development requires that we redefine the empirical claims of faith development in terms of the pragmatic functions of faith. I am more concerned with placing faith in the service of the self-world-transcendent relationship than with identifying an ideal universal community of faith (a "commonwealth of being") at stage six—though such might be desirable. It seems to me that the thrust of a developmental interpretation of faith is not to demonstrate its verb-like character or identify a specific endpoint in human development, but to show how faith functions in the dialectic of the temporal and the eternal. This requires a different theological anthropology, indeed, a fresh metaphor of the self—one that incorporates the transformations of the self as it confronts the paradoxes of existence. A dialectical-paradoxical hermeneutic of faith development interprets the history of the human subject not only as the history of progressive transformation but also as the history of suffering and negation.

Niebuhr prophetically calls human beings to respond to their true vocation as trustworthy and loyal participants in a triadic covenant that was initiated by God, the Creator, Governor, and Redeemer. His images of the human as *Homo dialogicus* and *Homo poeta* presume that social harmony will triumph over chaos and that God's presence in Jesus the Christ inspires us to recognize that authentic selfhood is constituted only in relation to an ever-widening nexus of moral relationships and responsibilities.

While I find some consolation in Niebuhr's optimistic belief that all things come together in a coherent universe under the sovereignty of God, I must question his theological anthropology from the perspective of the moral imperative for solidarity with victims of oppression throughout the world. Niebuhr read history through the eyes of American pragmatism and progressivism. He believed that meaning could arise from social interaction and that normative "I-Thou" relationships are possible. The principal threats to social harmony are "chaotic pluralism" and its accompanying moral relativism.

Those for whom the historical basis of faith is the underside of history cannot be so optimistic about faith on earth. For them the threat to the quest for meaning is, undoubtedly, the history of human suffering. Suffering ruptures the flow of progressivist theology and psychology. Suffering is the arena in which we are radically challenged to make sense of what it means to be human, what it means to be authentic selves before God.

The credibility of faith development theory will rest primarily on the ability of the theory to incorporate painful, tragic, and disjunctive phenomena, which threaten our imaging of ourselves as persons created in and called into a covenantal relationship with God and with God's creation. Here I note

Niebuhr's criticism of Kierkegaard's inattention to the social-historical conditions of relationality.[14] On the contrary, I suggest that Kierkegaard is not only extremely sensitive to this existential state of affairs but also illumines its dialectical and paradoxical nature.

DIALECTIC AND SOCIAL TRANSFORMATION

The attention of dialectical psychology to transformations in the self-world relationship introduces into our discussion the need for a critique of domination and an emancipatory praxis. Attention to the socio-political situation will certainly shed light on arenas of social interaction that obstruct or negate the structuring of meaning. The voices of those who do not fit into the established models of the good and the right need to be heard. For too long psychologists have formulated theories of human behavior that have ignored or distorted the experience of women, blacks, and other ethnic groups. This is precisely Carol Gilligan's argument in her book *In a Different Voice: Psychological Theory and Women's Development.*[15] Gilligan's concerns about the omission of women's voices need to be extended to other voices.

I agonize especially over the plight of America's black youth as political and economic conditions continue to contribute to the deterioration of a mass of humanity. In his book *The Truly Disadvantaged,* William Julius Wilson details the tragic circumstances under which America's youth in urban ghettos exist.[16] With an increasing number of youth living in single-parent households, the traditional nuclear family is in jeopardy. Furthermore, Wilson's data indicate that the chances of these families remaining in poverty are greater among households that are headed by females. The climate of basic trust between child and environment put forward by Erikson and Fowler as the norm of human development is being eroded by the forces of unemployment, poverty, racism, and narcotics. Erikson's "negative identity" is fast becoming the norm for America's black youth in the inner cities.

These realities point to the need for a broad ecological view of the world as a realm of multiple forces and relations that do not necessarily bring about the resolution of conflict, synergy, or the attainment of higher stages of meaning. This is not to say that human beings do not seek some kind of meaningful balance or synchrony within the temporal constraints of the life cycle. I am simply arguing that the quest for meaning and truth and the quest for freedom are inseparable. And so, I applaud the efforts of liberation and political theologians

> to understand how faith as narrative knowledge born of love, revealing the Divine anamnestic solidarity with all the lowly, redeems human reason and experience from the irrationalities of instrumentalist and other deformations of reason which have distorted rational praxis into modern forms of scientism, wherein knowledge becomes dominative power generated by fear.[17]

To summarize this chapter, dialectical psychology joins metaphorical theology in setting forth a framework for interdisciplinary interpretation of the transformation of self and world. Attention needs to be paid foremost to what we consider to be normative forms of self-world equilibrium. What we perceive as integration, particularly as an equilibrated stage, is more likely the result of action taken in response to crises and doubts, which are themselves indicative of the absence of synchrony in inner or outer relations. Action to achieve synchrony creates the conditions that lead to further imbalance. In other words, what we take to be wholeness might very well be a defensive posture against alienation. What is secure in one arena of life is merely a temporary platform for attending to discontinuities in other arenas. We have to remain open to new challenges, which can radically undo the gains made in one domain or another. Admittedly, this sounds very much like the myth of Sisyphus. But I am not advocating the utter meaninglessness of existence. I am simply agreeing with dialectical psychologists that change requires action on the world and that such action inevitably creates the need for further action in some other arena of life.

This is particularly difficult in the religious and moral domains. Crises and contradictions persist in spite of our valiant efforts to do the right thing and to live morally and spiritually integrated lives. In the moral domain, stability is perceived as moral consistency. We attempt to find rules or principles that are absolute and universal. And so, we find deontological ethics most appropriate. In the religious domain, the *magisterium* holds sway. Doctrines are made absolute, rabid fundamentalism persists, and unquestioned obedience is demanded by the *magisterium*.

The truth of the matter is that there is no enduring stability in every aspect of our lives. For the most part, we survive by making temporary truces in conflicting areas of personal and public life. It is hard to admit that the perimeters of meaning are not as comprehensive as we would like them to be. In an ideal world the multiple constituencies that demand our trust and fidelity would co-exist in perfect harmony. But we have to be realistic. Most of us live with conflicting loyalties and our pilgrimage along life's way is a series of tactical maneuvers to stave off chaos and anomie.

Dialectical psychology injects a refreshing realism into our quest for meaning by demanding that we be clear about the changes we seek in our lives and those aspects of our lives that we want to remain constant. Although I appreciate its realism, dialectical psychology locks us into a world of immanentalism. Accordingly, change appears as an end in itself and the empirical or material world is regarded as the ultimate reference of self-understanding.

I understand the ordering of life as life's relation to a transcendent ordering agent. Thus, the past, present, and future are situated in relation to eternal life. The tentativeness of life, which dialectical psychology emulates, prompts a deeper questioning of the dialectic of the temporal and the eternal. The concept of synchrony takes on new meaning as those aspects of our lives which fit together in a coherent whole—for example, work, family, and faith—are viewed in relation to the eternal. In other words, changes in our lives are punctuated by the belief that human history is ultimately made relative by God's final transformation of history.

CHAPTER FOUR

ARCHETYPAL TRANSFORMATIONS

No man can change himself into anything from sheer reason; he can only change into what he potentially is. When such a change becomes necessary, the previous mode of adaptation, already in a state of decay, is unconsciously compensated by the archetype of another mode.

—Carl Jung[1]

This chapter investigates Jung's project of *apocatastasis*—recovering the wholeness of the human condition. The central argument to be developed is that religious transformation is a process of being reconnected to the paradoxical wholeness of the *imago Dei*.

Analytical psychology is both teleological and paradoxical. Jung asserts that his psychological observations confirm that the psyche is structured as a union of opposites, a *coniunctio oppositorum*, the integration of which is the goal of personality development. A related assumption is that the meaningfulness of life rests on the recovery of its primordial wholeness.

The archetypes of the collective or transpersonal unconscious are the psychological matrix linking the individual pursuit of meaning to humanity's original condition of wholeness. These archetypes provide images and symbols of what humanity was in the beginning of time *(in illo tempore)* and what it ought to become. These images and symbols reflect the paradoxical structure of reality—the opposites of light and darkness, good

73

and evil, masculine and feminine, and so on, and their reconciliation as a *coincidentia oppositorum*.

The antinomies that define the structure of the psyche are considered the vectors along which the quest for wholeness occurs. In the Jungian paradigm, paradox is "a system of value" through which the psyche and reality itself are organized. I take my definition of a paradoxical system of value from Karl Plank.

> The paradoxical system of value has an elusiveness which springs from the heart of its ongoing movement. Such a system can only be elusive for, by nature, paradoxes are "self-consuming," unable to stay at rest or halt the movement they begin.[2]

Of particular importance is the contrariety of paradox.

> A paradox can become a definition, a source of expectation, only at a loss of its essential contrariety. In receiving reality as ordered by this paradoxical movement one still recognizes a structured world but, at the same time, takes heed of its provisional nature.[3]

In analytical psychology, reality is ordered by a paradoxical movement of archetypal polarities. Individuation is the process by which these polarities are integrated. In this process, the ego, the center of awareness, differentiates from the Self—the center of wholeness—and reintegrates with the Self over the course of the life history. Jung maintains that it is in mid-life that we are mature enough to take on the arduous task of integrating the negative and contrasexual opposites of the personality.

ARCHETYPES AND INDIVIDUATION

Jung drew extensively on philosophy, religion, mythology, and other disciplines to formulate his hypotheses and theoretical conclusions. The concept of the archetype has moved through various formulations and continues to be debated among Jungians. Generally speaking, there are two standard versions—the psychoid archetype as an actual pre-existent form, and the archetype as an image or symbol of a pre-existent form. The psychoid archetype is the more controversial. It expresses the metaphysical unity of psyche and world. On the basis of this formulation, Jung addresses the numinosity of the archetypes and their function in the evolution of moral and religious meaning.

The principal archetypes of the personality are the *persona* or mask that is presented to the external world and its opposite, the *shadow* or negative side. The *animus* is the masculine archetype in the woman. Its contrasexual opposite is the *anima*, the feminine archetype in the male. What constitutes masculine and feminine archetypes is highly debatable. Jung relied on Victorian stereotypes of masculine and feminine to supply the imagery for contrasexual integration. Not surprising, he is criticized for his sexist views of the feminine.[4]

He portrays the woman as helpmate, consort, and counterplayer to the aggressive, dominant male. Elevating the woman to the status of goddess does not negate the marginality of the feminine in patriarchal religion and culture.[5]

To make matters worse, several of Jung's female disciples have reiterated his views of the independently minded, "animus-ridden" woman who rebels against her nature and refuses to nurture the man's anima, the source of his creativity.[6] Woman's independent creativity is looked upon as exceptional. Creativity, if at all recognized, is confined to child-bearing.

Influenced by Platonic Idealism, Jung promotes the existence of two archetypally determined principles of masculine and feminine functioning, both of which exist in persons of either sex. The Logos principle is the masculine, rational, intellectual function. Its opposite is Eros, the affective, relational principle. The wholeness of the personality is marked by the union of Logos and Eros. Despite the ideal of contrasexual union, the feminine is undervalued. The animus is simply derived from the anima.

At a time when men and women are revolting against absolute norms of sexual relations, the notion of the contrasexual union of opposites is especially controversial. The logical expression of contrasexual union is the androgyne. But is androgyny any more real than the unicorn? As homosexuality becomes more prominent as an alternative life-style, the question of normative sexuality becomes increasingly ambiguous. The ideal of the androgyne is made even more complex by advances in medical technology. Transsexual operations make it difficult to determine who is male or female. Thus some church leaders recommend that sexuality be considered a nonmoral issue.[7]

If we are to preserve the paradoxicality of sexual wholeness, then we have to be openminded about its embodiment in homosexuals. Jung's paradoxical system of value introjects into human sexuality a necessary tentativeness. Our perceptions of wholeness whether in the heterosexual or homosexual are always tempered by the presence of the contrary. Hence, it is just as one-sided to promote gynecentric worship of the goddess as it is to perpetuate androcentrism. The politicization of sexuality in the Church makes it difficult to find models of God that express the paradoxical wholeness of human sexuality.[8]

The paradoxical system of value is intended to widen our perceptions of reality beyond the one-sidedness of ego consciousness by drawing on the symbols and images from the collective unconscious. Jungian psychotherapists would most likely insist that the integration of the collective unconscious requires intensive analytical psychotherapy. Only then can we subject the paradoxical union of opposites to a continuing process of interpretation, and integrate the complexity of dreams and other symbols into the process of individuation.

I do not dispute the benefits of psychotherapy but will insist that the significance of Jung's ideas is not limited to their psychotherapeutic applications. Analytical psychology is primarily concerned with the experience of meaning, and, as Aniela Jaffe points out, "The experience of meaning depends on the awareness of a transcendental or spiritual reality that complements the empirical reality of life and together with it forms a whole."[9] It is impossible to find moral and religious meaning in our lives without deliberately seeking the recovery of wholeness.

MEANING AND THE NUMINOUS

Jung suggests that the psychoid unconscious is both a source of new life and a repository of destructive forces. It is a place to which the psyche regresses and from which new meaning emanates. In the descent of Jonah into the bowels of the fish, Jung found a classic narrative of the paradox of death and life in the psychoid unconscious. Jonah's escape from the world of consciousness into the depths of darkness is paradoxically an occasion for entering into a new form of life. The test of this experience is the ego's ability to assimilate insights from the psychoid unconscious. Schizophrenia is a pathological splitting of the psyche. The psychotherapeutic implications of assimilating or not assimilating the contents of the psychoid unconscious, though important, are not our immediate concern. Rather, the issue at hand is the numinosity of the psychoid unconscious. Jung asserts that we are grasped by a primal power from deep within the psyche that corresponds to the experience of the holy. The numinosity of the experience of God and that of the psychoid unconscious is the basis of Jung's argument that subjective experiences of the Self and God are indistinguishable. Both the Self and God are archetypal representations of an unknown transcendental reality.[10]

> This is not to say that what we call the unconscious is identical with God or is set up in his place. It is simply the medium from which religious experience seems to flow. As to what the further case of such experience may be, the answer to this lies beyond the range of human knowledge. Knowledge of God is a transcendental problem.[11]

Jung leaves it up to theologians and philosophers to speculate on the nature of God. Yet, his epistemology is colored by Platonism. We know God only through the numinosity of the God-image. It makes no difference whether the *numen* is encountered in a dream or in culture. For example, the mandala functions in dreams and myths as a symbol of the Self but is also ritualized in Hinduism as a symbol of wholeness in the circumambulation of the holy city of Vanarsi (Benares). What matters is the creative function of consciousness in assimilating the numinosity of the *imago Dei*. The imagination is entirely dependent on the contents of the unconscious for moral and religious meaning. Jung's idea of a cosmically oriented moral imagination is appropriate for our present efforts to widen the horizons of responsibility for the preservation of the ecosystem. The image of God emerging from the collective unconscious directs our imagination to the wholeness of creation. The unconscious reveals to us images of God that have become inscribed in myths of creation and rebirth. In these myths we find the opposites of anima and animus, good and evil, light and darkness, life and death.

For Christians, the renewal of human life depends on the relation to Christ. The *imago Dei* in Christ is the paradigm for the restoration of wholeness. This wholeness *(shalom)* is precisely what the resurrected Christ bequeathed to his disciples—"Peace be with you" (John 20:19). In the sacrament of holy baptism, we declare our acceptance of the transforming presence of the Holy Spirit. This paradoxical rite of death and rebirth marks the beginning of the conversion of the imagination to the wholeness of Christ. Our greatest problem is to sustain this conversion in a fragmented world.

Without devaluing the importance of believing that the Holy Spirit sustains our conversion to Christ, the process of individuation depicts the conversion to Christ as a continuing process of confronting the polarities of the psyche which corrupt the *imago Dei* and restoring the *imago Dei* to its wholeness. Crucial to this restoration is the assimilation of the contrasexual and shadow archetypes. Both of these create considerable difficulties for the contemporary Church. The shadow archetype will be taken up in the next section. The matter of contrasexual integration in the *imago Dei* warrants more extensive treatment than is possible at this time. Suffice it to say, accepting the feminine and masculine on equal terms is firmly rejected by several religious denominations. The feminine remains repressed and underdeveloped. The opportunity for infusing the Church and the world with new life is lost as women are denied their calling to the ordained ministry.

The collective unconscious continues to produce images of wholeness for the Church that threaten the power-wielders. The obsessive resistance to women as bearers of the wholeness of the *imago Dei* fosters *enantiodromia.* Jung adopted Heraclitus' principle of *enantiodromia* to describe the flow of psychic energy as a running of opposites into each other. In the individuation process, the conflict between archetypal opposites can be such that we try to establish artificial boundaries between them. The more we try to impose conscious boundaries, the more the compensatory action of the unconscious psyche brings about a contrary movement. The masculinization of the Church is a case in point. The failure of the power-wielders in the Church to recognize the equivalency of the masculine and the feminine in the *imago Dei* has left us in the throes of *enantiodromia*. The feminine has arisen with such force that it is futile to deny women their vocation to reenact sacramentally the paradoxical wholeness of the body of Christ.

EVIL AND THE *IMAGO DEI*

Far more complex than the integration of the contrasexual opposites in the *imago Dei* is the integration of good and evil.

Jung interprets the story of Job as a classic case of Job's consciousness of God as Redeemer and Destroyer.[12] In the debate between Job and God, God realizes that Job is aware of these conflicting qualities. Satan appears as one of God's sons who acts as an adversary of God. Satan elicits the dualities of God's nature. For Jung, the central issue in this narrative is Job's ability to reconcile these conflicting dualities in God's identity without losing his faith in God's redemptive power. These contradictions do not weaken God's power, nor do they diminish Job's faith.

What troubles theologians about Jung's interpretation of this narrative is his assertion that the Incarnation is God's answer to Job. God humanizes the conflicting dualities of good and evil in the Godhead by becoming incarnate in Christ. Jung suggests that in the historical development of Christianity, good and evil became personified as an apocalyptic battle between Christ and the Antichrist.

It is not difficult to understand why *Answer to Job* provoked considerable controversy. In the eyes of some critics, Jung's reading of Job and of the Incarnation was nothing short of heresy. From the early Church fathers (no wonder there is such one-sidedness in Christianity), Christians have been trying to figure out how to reconcile the polarities of good and evil with God's identity as Creator and Redeemer. Origen, Augustine, and others maintained that evil is the *steresis* or privation of the good *(privatio boni)*. God exists as the greatest good *(summum bonum)*.

Jung felt that doctrinal separations of these polarities were inconsistent with what he had observed in the experiences of his patients and with what he himself had experienced.[13] The question is not whether God created evil or is responsible for evil but whether evil is an integral feature of the *imago Dei*. Jung criticizes Christians for creating a specious bifurcation of good and evil in the *imago Dei* incarnate in Christ. Christians confuse the wholeness of Christ with moral perfection, and evil with the lack of perfection.

Jung insists that he writes as a clinician and not as a theologian. Accordingly, his views on evil are grounded in his clinical analysis of the shadow archetype. However, the relation of evil to the shadow is ambiguous. The shadow archetype in the personal unconscious is not necessarily evil. It includes the repressed, suppressed, and unintegrated negative aspects of the personal unconscious. But there is also a collective unconscious dimension to the shadow. Evil is an acting out of humanity's negative forces, resulting in the psychic suffering of humanity in general.

If repentance is the starting point of conversion to Christ, then, for Jung, the restoration of evil to its proper place in the *imago Dei* is the beginning of the conversion of the imagination to Christ.

> This is in exact agreement with the empirical findings of psychology, that there is an ever-present archetype of wholeness which may disappear from the purview of consciousness or may never be perceived at all until a consciousness illuminated by conversion recognizes it in the figure of Christ. As a result of this *anamnesis* the original state of oneness with the God-image is restored.[14]

Jung's use of the term *anamnesis* to denote the recovery of primordial wholeness is relevant to our later discussion of

Kierkegaard's concept of repetition. Jung is so rooted in the numinosity of the archetype that he treats conversion as a mystical transformational experience—an ecstatic illumination of the Self, which by definition includes the shadow archetype. Since Jung adopts a teleological perspective on the evolution of consciousness, it follows that meaning is also to be found in the experience of God's dark side. Jung drew on mystics such as Jakob Böhme and Meister Eckhart to support his argument that the experience of God's shadow side is pivotal to our understanding of God's redemptive work in Christ. Perhaps this is what John of the Cross experienced as the "dark night of the soul"—the inseparability of God's shadow and God's love. We find similar paradoxes in the experiences of Abraham as he obeyed God's command to sacrifice Isaac, and in Job's faithfulness in the midst of his suffering. Jung's interpretation of the Job narrative is strikingly similar to James' view of the strenuous mood and its relation to God's salvific action. The latter is to be tested in the storm and stress of the moral life. Here we encounter God's shadow side but also new possibilities of wholeness, which may "transcend the one-sidedness of the spirit of the time and prepare the way for a transformation."[15]

I find Jung's honesty about the difficult paradoxes of Christian faith refreshing. Even the most pious and righteous Christian experiences the irreducible paradox of good and evil in the *imago Dei*. Lucifer, from the Latin *lux* (light) and *ferre* (to bear), is both prince of darkness and bearer of light. "The real devil first appears as the adversary of Christ, and with him we gaze for the first time into the luminous realm of divinity on the one hand and into the abyss of hell on the other."[16]

Jung is certainly not advocating satanism. Satanism is a rejection of the wholeness of God. However, Jung's experiential approach to religion prevents him from distinguishing clearly between idolatry and genuine worship of God. God is whatever we experience as an "overpowering psychic factor."[17]

I must admit my dissatisfaction with Jung's emphasis on numinosity as the experiential basis of the divine and the demonic. In the unconscious, these are indistinguishable, so we do not know which of them predominates. And so Jung concludes that all we can do is hope that good, namely "what seems fitting to us will prevail."[18]

The test of healthy religion, then, is its ability to assimilate the psychic antithesis of good and evil in the *imago Dei* and in human nature. Christianity's paradox is that the one who embodies the wholeness of God becomes the victim of humanity's dark side. In redeeming humanity, the unblemished goodness of Christ shows up humanity's dark side. But, according to Jung, since Christ is fully human and fully divine, Christians should acknowledge the polarities of good and evil in the Christ archetype. Instead, Christians have spiritualized Christ and excluded the instinctual, bodily aspects of Christ from the Christ image.

A similar situation exists in the doctrine of the Trinity. A fourth principle is missing. Jung finds support for this missing element in medieval alchemy. The alchemical concept of the *quaternio* is considered a paradigm of the integration of opposites. In light of the *quaternio,* there is an imbalance in the Trinity. Whether this alleged imbalance is rectified by the inclusion of the shadow archetype or the feminine archetype remains unclear.[19] According to Jung's psychological hermeneutic, the Holy Spirit is an unmediated unifying force at work in the world, uniting the spiritual and material, and transforming the world toward greater wholeness. An obvious criticism of this position is that Jung fails to recognize that the distortion of the God-image, that is, the wholeness of God, is due to sin. It is this understanding of human sin that creates a discrepancy between the wholeness intended by natural propensities of the psyche and that intended by God.

In addition, Jung does not distinguish between opposites that are contradictory and those that are contrary. Robert Doran attributes this confusion to two types of transpersonal symbols in analytical psychology, archetypal and anagogic. Archetypal symbols reflect the conflict within the psyche and the process of integration, for example, the contrasexual opposites. Anagogic symbols reflect the participation of the person in contradictory opposites that are irreconcilable, such as good and evil.

The dialectic of the subject is a dialectic of contraries. The dialectic of good and evil is a dialectic of contradictories. A dialectic of contraries is resolved by allotting each pole its due place. A dialectic of contradictories is resolved only by affirming one pole and negating the opposite. One cannot without contradiction both promote and displace the integral dialectic of the subject. To promote it is good, to displace it is evil: one must choose.[20]

Doran strikes at the core of the process of individuation. Jung places so much confidence in the psyche's ability to balance the needs of the ego and the resources of the unconscious that intentionality is easily overlooked. Doran not only illumines the role of choice in resolving the contrariety of good and evil, he also places this dialectic in its proper perspective, namely, in relation to the transformation of humanity and the world. For Jung, archetypal symbols are elements of nature. They imitate the dialectic of limitation and transcendence in nature. In contrast, Doran maintains that even when anagogic symbols are derived from nature, as in the classic poem in Isaiah 11:6-9, which tells of antagonists lying in peace with each other, they are directed to "nature's re-creation and transformation."[21]

Much more needs to be said about Jung's psychological interpretation of Christianity, but this would take us beyond the scope of this study. It is enough to say that Jung's explorations of Christianity's contribution to the wholeness of humanity led him not only to discover links between Christianity and alchemy but also to retrieve Christianity's early connections with Gnosticism.[22] Here again, in establishing empirical support for his psychological hermeneutic, Jung trivializes the theological significance of the early Church's rejection of Gnosticism. The point is that Gnosticism rejected the continuity of the God of Judaism and the God of Jesus Christ. Jung does not delve into the deeper theological foundations of Christianity. He limits his interpretation of Christianity to its symbolic value. In short, he treats the symbolic value of religion as if it were the governing principle of religious life.

Moreover, he concentrates on a particular formulation of values, namely, those which contribute to the integration of the personality, as evidenced by symbols of transformation and rebirth. The symbolic value of Christ is that he is the Redeemer who restores humanity to a right relationship with God. The crucifixion is seen as the ultimate act of vicarious suffering.

To summarize this part of our discussion, Jung sees the Christian vocation as the *imitatio Christi*, the chief characteristic of which is vicarious suffering. The paradox of imitating Christ is that one has to die in order to be born anew. In translating this reshaping and re-formation of the human in the image of Christ as a journey into the awesome darkness of the shadow, Jung enlightens our consciousness of the hard paradoxes of Christian faith and "the metamorphosis of grace."[23]

PRESENCE AND ABSENCE

The discovery of grace in the dark night of the soul lends credibility to the eschatological hope that good will ultimately triumph over evil. From Jung's point of view, humanity is moving toward the imaginative appropriation of the wholeness of creation in the *imago Dei*. This is not to imply that Jung was insensitive to the horrors of human suffering. On the contrary, he was deeply moved by the suffering of humanity during the Second World War. He acknowledged that suffering was indeed the way of the cross. Yet, he did not seem to realize that the suffering of the world is more important to Christianity than doctrines of Christ's identity. He paid more attention to the doctrine of the Trinity as a statement on the integration of archetypal opposites in the *imago Dei* than to its articulation of God's eternal participation in the suffering of the world.

He emphasized the polarities that are concerned with the identity of God and Christ—the kind of opposites John Skorupski calls "paradoxes of identity."[24] These have to do with how Christ can suffer and be God at the same time, how evil and good can co-exist in the Christ-image, and so on.

Jung approaches the doctrine of the Trinity as a paradox of identity. For my part, this doctrine speaks to God's continuing transformation of the world. If there is something missing from the doctrine, it has nothing to do with the completion of a quaternity but with the paradox of presence and absence. This is poignantly expressed by the apostle Paul. To the Corinthians, Paul's afflictions signified the absence of God. To Paul, they afforded him an opportunity to participate in God's restoration of the wholeness of creation.

The paradox of presence and absence is not concerned with the presence or absence of evil in the *imago Dei* but with God's identification with the suffering of the world. According to Jung's paradox of identity, only a God whose nature includes evil is able to take on the suffering of the world. This is why God is to be loved as well as feared. Here again, Jung's God is an archetype that is derived from and imitates nature. Jung's natural theology leaves God trapped in immanence. Jung would have us believe that even in the worst experiences of evil it is possible to experience the archetype of wholeness and that suffering is alleviated by the discovery of this wholeness. This optimism sounds fine, but does it make sense to victims? The victim's liberation rests on the ability to keep the dialectic of good and evil in a harmonious balance. In a word, suffering is sublated to the integrated self.

In shifting the axis of good and evil from the psyche to the person, Doran adopts a radically different approach to paradox. Instead of the both-and paradox of archetypal opposites, we have an either-or paradox of good and evil. For victims, this means that their freedom is not cast in the psychic domain of dialectically balanced opposites but in the moral domain where the person is up against hard choices and exigencies that "can be met *or* declined, but that cannot be both met *and* declined."[25] Anagogic symbols emerge from and give meaning to the hard paradoxes of existence. Doran calls these symbols anagogic since they reflect "the orientation to the transcendent mystery whose grace is the condition of the possibility of the resolution of the dialectic of good and evil."[26] Their redemptive or soteriological value is of primary importance to victims. Put differently, at stake is our ability to discover, in the hard choices and exigencies of life, God's continuing redemption of the world. Whereas Jung underscores the wholeness of creation, Doran illumines God's redemption and transformation of creation. In the latter case, good and evil are not contrary opposites to be integrated into an overarching whole. Rather what qualifies as good is what fosters the integration of the psyche; similarly, evil is what negates the harmonious integration of opposites.

This turn toward anagogic symbols has profound implications for Christianity. For one thing, what is at stake is not the transformation of the psyche but the transformation of the person. Pertinent to the latter is the issue of tragedy. The temptation is to diminish the horror of tragedy and evil by subsuming it to a monistic or overarching whole. This, in Brian Hebblethwaite's opinion, is contrary to Christian faith. According to Hebblethwaite, the genius of Christian faith is its proclamation that nothing is beyond redemption. The gospel is not about integration of opposites but about their transformation and redemption. Christians are called to preach

> a gospel of redemption whereby the world's sorrow will be turned into joy and the inevitable sufferings and travail of the present phase of God's creative purpose will give birth to a glory beyond compare. That must mean a glory in which both victims and perpetrators (the former made new and whole and the latter transformed and forgiven) participate. Such a consummation may or may not occur. But Christianity is committed to the faith that it will occur.[27]

In summary, Jung's emphasis on archetypal wholeness leaves us in search of the hidden God *(deus absconditus)* in the psyche and nature.[28] The either-or paradoxes of the moral life are sublated to the both-and paradoxes of archetypal wholeness. This leaves a serious lacuna in the formation of Christian faith and identity. The cross of Christ is "an icon of paradox."[29] It embraces both-and and either-or. It symbolizes God's identifying with the weak and bringing strength from weakness. Christ, in his crucifixion, fully embraced the darkness of sin and evil but in his resurrection gave to humanity a clear choice of new life over death, the profundity of which Nicodemus could not comprehend (John 3:1-10). The either-or paradox of good and evil impressed upon us by the resurrected Christ places moral choice at the center of our becoming formed in the image of Christ. The eschatological hope is that in the end all humanity will *choose* the new life given by Christ. Until then, the Christ image will reflect a perfected creation or wholeness that is yet to come.

In the final analysis, while Jung sharpens our consciousness of the irreducible paradoxes of Christianity, his invitation to wholeness is not an invitation to Christian discipleship. It is an invitation to become transformed by the mysterious power of the transpersonal unconscious, whence emanate images of humanity's primordial wholeness in the *imago Dei* as well as images of rebirth in Christ. How these images take shape in our lives is dictated by the moral choices that we make in seeking to become like Christ. Among these choices is the inescapable choice of the cross. How this choice becomes an open-ended journey into the darkness of humanity and a re-birth of God's self-emptying love in the world will be taken up in the next chapter.

CHAPTER FIVE

BECOMING A SELF
BEFORE GOD

I am myself again.

—Søren Kierkegaard

Kierkegaard's attention to the interiority of the self leads dialectically to the existential situation within which authentic selfhood is formed.

Most scholars would agree that Kierkegaard's explication of the self through his pseudonyms is a *tour de force*. Climacus (the climber) offers a somewhat tortuous dialectical exposition of movement through the spheres of existence. His intense penetration of Hegelian philosophy is a *via negativa* through which its limitations are disclosed. These limitations include the idea of Christianity as a historical process. Climacus' astute philosophical speculations in *Philosophical Fragments* and in the *Concluding Unscientific Postscript* are a necessary background for viewing the theological observations and religious sensibilities of Anti-Climacus, the author of *The Sickness unto Death*, and the paradoxical musings of Constantin Constantius, author of *Repetition*. My primary focus in this chapter is on the concept of repetition and its implications for the transformation of existence.

We begin with a brief exposition of Kierkegaard's concept of the self. According to Kierkegaard, the self is a synthesis of the temporal and the eternal, the finite and the infinite, necessity and possibility. This synthesis is not simply a unity of body and soul, the physical and the psychological. Such a relationship does not demand responsibility or choice on the part of the self. It is a passive relationship, grounded in the immediacy of the moment. It exists in despair "over the earthly or over something earthly."[1] As such, the "self" does not exist.

> The appearance of such words as "the self" and "despair" in the language of immediacy is due, if you will, to an innocent abuse of language, a playing with words, like the children's game of playing soldier.[2]

This "self" that is not really a self is devoid of reflection. Caught in the dialectic of "the pleasant and the unpleasant," this creature of immediacy surrenders to fate and chance.[3]

Authentic selfhood requires critical reflection. There is a shift from being acted on by the world to acting on the world. The question arises whether the self is constituted autonomously or by another. With the capacity for reflection comes despair—the "despair of weakness" and the "despair of defiance." In the former, the individual lacks the will to take on the demands of existence. He or she settles for constancy and security in an untroubled existence. In the "despair of defiance," the individual refuses to acknowledge the spiritual power that unites body and soul and brings about the transformation of the self. The individual would rather live in a world of fantasy than respond to the demands of a spiritually transformed existence.

> In spite of all his despair, however, he cannot manage to do it; in spite of all his despairing efforts, that power is the stronger and forces him to be the self he does not want to be. But this is his way of willing to get rid of himself, to rid himself of the self that he is in order to be the self that he has dreamed up. He would be in seventh heaven to be the self he wants to be (although in another sense he would be just as despairing), but to be forced to be the self he does not want to be, that is his torment—that he cannot get rid of himself.[4]

Spirit unites as well as disturbs the relation of body and soul. "A human being is spirit. But what is spirit? Spirit is the self."[5]

89

Spirit is the synthesis of body and soul. This consciousness of the self as spirit is the basis from which we can speak of the moral and religious transformation of the self.

The forms of despair diagnosed by Kierkegaard reflect the various ways we fall short in our responses to the moral and religious demands of authentic selfhood. These include basing our selfhood on material existence, preoccupation with the illusions of an ideal existence, abysmal ignorance of possibilities for authentic selfhood, and demonic despair. The latter is most tragic for the despairing person who has abstracted himself or herself from concrete existence in the effort to will to be an autonomous self. Such a person is "afraid of eternity, afraid that it will separate him from his, demonically understood, infinite superiority over other men, his justification, demonically understood, for being what he is."[6]

The courage to respond to eternity is the measure of authentic selfhood. In other words, the eternal is the ultimate perspective from which to view the transformation of existence. But what is the eternal? And is it to be found in the past, present, or future?

RECOLLECTION AND REPETITION

Following Aristotle, Kierkegaard identified two types of change, namely *alloiosis,* a change in essence, and *kinesis,* a change in the mode of being or becoming. *Alloiosis* denotes the ability of the self to transcend its historical facticity through imaginative reflection. Such is to be found in Platonic recollection. The eternal is posited as a backward movement from the temporal. It is a pre-existent ideal moment that has been lost. It is therefore a contradiction.

> Recollection is not ideality; it is ideality that has been. It is not reality; it is reality that has been—which again is a double contradiction, for ideality, according to its concept, cannot have been, and the same holds true of reality according to its concept.[7]

Simply put, recollection is directed toward the past. It offers nothing to the future but what has already existed.

Repetition is a crucial expression for what "recollection" was to the Greeks. Just as they taught that all knowing is a recollecting, modern philosophy will teach that all life is a repetition. . . . Repetition and recollection are the same movement, except in opposite directions, for what is recollected has been, is repeated backward, whereas genuine repetition is recollected forward. Repetition, therefore, if it is possible, makes a person happy, whereas recollection makes him unhappy—assuming, of course, that he gives himself time to live and does not promptly at birth find an excuse to sneak out of life again, for example, that he has forgotten something.[8]

The polemic of recollection versus repetition is not simply a metaphysical problem. Rather, it is concerned with the very nature of existence itself. Recollection is indicative of the human propensity to find ways of escaping from the demands and responsibilities of existence—to recollect oneself out of time itself. Kierkegaard notes that even Aristotle resisted the temptation of Platonic recollection, to seek the Ideal in the past. Aristotle opted instead for *kinesis*—"the transition from possibility to actuality."[9] Possibility belongs to the future, not to the past. Our problem is to live with the changes necessary for the future. It is so much easier to retreat into the past.

How then do we make the changes necessary for the future? In other words, how do we live as if we are still "coming into existence"? Kierkegaard suggests that we do so by repetition. *Repetition* (Danish, *Gjentagelsen*) is a metaphor for the enduring reality of the self in the midst of change. Its philosophical intent is to reconcile the Eleatic concept of static being and the Heraclitian concept of endless flux. It considers the human as being in the process of becoming.

The dialectic of repetition is easy, for that which is repeated has been—otherwise it could not be repeated—but the very fact that it has been makes the repetition into something new. When the Greeks said that all knowing is recollecting, they said that all existence which is, has been; when one says that life is a repetition, one says: actuality, which has been, now comes into existence. If one does not have the category of recollection or of repetition, all life dissolves into an empty, meaningless noise.[10]

The process of "coming into existence" involves one's past, present, and future. As a way of relating to the past, recollection is ideal. We use it to determine how we relate to the present and our hope for the future. Hope, grounded in recollection, is mere speculation—"a beckoning fruit that does not satisfy."[11] This is characteristic of the aesthete who longs for a future that is nothing more than a repetition of the past.

I should interject that this was Kierkegaard's personal experience. The book *Repetition* alludes to his loss of Regine. Fleeing to Berlin, Kierkegaard poetically cast the *angst* of separation and loss in the dialectic of time and eternity. The protagonists in this romantic *novella* are a nameless young man and Constantin Constantius, the paragon of stability. The young man compares his suffering owing to his loss of love to that of Job, and hopes to recover himself as Job did. His hope is mired in the past, the locus of his constancy—a point not missed by Constantin Constantius.

> Recollection has the great advantage that it begins with the loss; the reason it is safe and secure is that it has nothing to lose.[12]

The past is already lost. But this is the source of the young man's melancholy. In vain, Constantius tries to direct his attention to changes in the environment.

> Neither the broad bold assurance of the sea nor the hushed silence of the forest nor the beckoning solitude of the evening could bring him out of the melancholy longing in which he not so much drew near to the beloved as withdrew from her. His mistake was incurable, and his mistake was that he stood at the end instead of at the beginning, but such a mistake is and remains a person's downfall.[13]

As a metaphor from the theater, repetition is a "retaking" or repeating what was previously enacted as if it were for the first time. The young man seeks to recover lost love. But repetition is not merely the recovery of lost love. It is the recovery of lost selfhood, and selfhood is *essentially* a dialectical relation between the finite and the infinite. This relation is constituted not by the self but by the eternal Power upon which the self rests. Sin is the result of defiantly rejecting this relationship. The relationship is recovered only by repentance and forgiveness. The self is also *existentially* a relation between necessity and possibility, between what it has become in existing and what it is yet to become. This is the "battle of faith"—to believe that "with God everything is possible."[14]

To continue the drama, the young man seeks a form of life or quality of selfhood in which the temporal is endowed with the eternal. He seeks constancy in the midst of change, in the form of eternal love. But such love is given only by God. It does not evolve by a natural historical process and is not determined by the dialectic logic of Hegel's philosophy.

This drama takes us through aesthetic, ethical, and religious forms of repetition. Through them, we glimpse the existential transformation of the self. The dynamics of this transformation are complex. Repetition is not change for the sake of change. It has to do with the passions and interests that shape authentic selfhood. We have to understand then how repetition takes hold of a person's life, how it involves the transition to a more authentic form of life. In short, "Genuine repetition is— earnestness."[15] This sounds very much like James' strenuous mood. However, in contrast to James, the God-relationship is not a cooperative union of wills. This relationship is a paradox. The Incarnation is the Absolute Paradox. The existential pathos of the finite-infinite relationship comes from the absurd unity of the temporal and the eternal.

Religiously understood, to exist in relation to the infinite is to become a self before God. This means living with the awareness that "against God we are always in the wrong."[16] This guilt-consciousness is dialectically related to the consciousness of the eternal blessedness or happiness *(Salighed)* of being in the God-relationship.[17]

The earnestness of repetition is a concentrated passion for rebirth. This entails decisive moral action. That is to say, the self must will the absolute good by which it is eternally transformed. And what is the absolute good? According to Abrahim Khan, it is eternal happiness *(Salighed)*.

For an individual to have an infinite interest in an eternal happiness he must acknowledge that happiness *(Salighed)*, as an absolute telos, is an ethical good for his life.[18]

Existence is transformed when an individual is related decisively to this absolute good and "is aware of being grasped by a deep *existential pathos* of the absurd."[19]

The *pathos* engendered by acknowledging an eternal happiness *(Salighed)* as the *absolute* good is not a matter of the *existing person's* having to express the pathos in words, but of his permitting the conception of the absolute good to transform his entire *existence.*[20]

We could say then that the concepts of *repetition* and *Salighed* are inextricably related. *Salighed* is the absolute telos toward which the transformation of selfhood is directed. This implies that the self is divided.[21] It is not what it ought to be. It is in a disrelation to the eternal, hence is in a state of guilt. On this point, Khan is very incisive.

To say that a person's true individuality is marked by guilt is to say, in effect, that a person confronted with the demand of *Salighed* recognizes what he is and what he can become ethically. That he experiences within himself an opposition which is the result of the self's requiring for its fulfillment an ideality not obtainable in time, namely, *Salighed.* As long as the self fails to take notice of the demands of *Salighed* it will continue to remain inauthentic and to negate itself.[22]

Noting the use of the concept *Salighed* by Climacus in the *Concluding Unscientific Postscript,* Khan underscores that

a person's true humanity depends on the exercise of his passional rather than his logical capacity. In other words, the concept *Salighed* belongs to that set of concepts having to do with the understanding of selfhood. It is part of a network of existential concepts that includes passion, infinite interest, pathos, guilt, and existence.[23]

The dominance of the passional over the rational is particularly pertinent to the belief in the Absolute Paradox, namely, the Incarnation. According to Khan, this contradiction of the eternal becoming temporal "has to be believed if one is to become properly related to *Salighed*. The reason is that the paradoxical nature of the datum requires of a person the highest possible passion, which *Salighed* demands, before belief is possible."[24]

To summarize, repetition is the reconstituting of the self's relation to the eternal. This is the fullest extent of what a person can become ethically and spiritually. According to Climacus, this absolute telos is *Salighed,* salvation or eternal happiness. In its striving, the self bears the guilt of being in disrelation to the eternal but is also driven by the belief that authentic selfhood is constituted only in relation to the eternal. This striving for eternal happiness is not the burden of the individual alone. In the Incarnation, God entered into human time. This act has transformed existence by bringing the temporal into its proper and authentic relation to the eternal. The earnestness of the individual in responding to this event is met by the grace of God.

With the absolute telos of authentic selfhood in mind, let us examine in greater detail the making of authentic selfhood in the aesthetic, ethical, and religious spheres of existence.

AESTHETIC REPETITION: FLOWING WITH TIME

In "The Rotation Method," Kierkegaard describes how the aesthete tries to arrange life into an orderly sequence of changes, as if life were a series of crops which matured in the flow of time. This is how the aesthete takes on the dialectic of the temporal and the eternal. The eternal is imagined as an endless protraction of the temporal. Selfhood flows with the flow of time. Order in the internal self is derived from order in the external world; hence, there is no existential imperative to cultivate inwardness.

Boredom is the aesthete's greatest fear. Faced with apparent unlimited pleasure, the aesthete is lost in a sea of immediate fulfillment. Ironically, novelty is gained not by one more experience of pleasure but by the decision to organize life as a farmer would rotate crops. This is futile. Alienation from the eternal persists in spite of order in the external world. Lacking inwardness, the aesthete is overcome by the despair of infinite possibilities. She or he is unable to make any substantial and longlasting choices. Marriage is perhaps the most difficult choice.

> If, instead of promising forever, the parties would say: until Easter, or until May-day comes, there might be some meaning in what they say; for then they would have said something definite, and also something they might be able to keep.[25]

Rotation then is repetition on the aesthetic level. It is the mark of a narcissistic hedonist who skillfully and deceptively uses his or her intellect to find authentic selfhood. Moral imperatives are construed in terms of instrumental utilitarianism. This is amplified in the essay "Diary of a Seducer" at the end of the first volume of *Either/Or,* where the seducer demonstrates his narcissistic skill of using women as extensions of himself. He dominates and treats them as though they were dependent on him for the development of self-consciousness. In the end, the dispassionate and cunning seducer is seduced by self-deception. The imagination serves as a medium of infinite possibility. The seducer's despair is that he lacks finitude. He has no sense of boundaries, hence, no sense of guilt. In actuality, he has no self, no "consciousness of existing before God."[26]

ETHICAL REPETITION: "CHOOSE THYSELF"

Fortunately, the aesthete's refined hedonism is not the extent of authentic selfhood. In the ethical sphere, he has to make difficult choices. Kierkegaard recasts the Socratic dictum "Know thyself" as "Choose thyself." The interiority of the self is at stake. Interiority is the incorporation of eternal values and principles, for example, love and justice. Governed by interiority, the ethical self takes on the conflicts and contradictions of the moral life.

This portrait of the ethical is fraught with the dual dangers of self-righteousness and moral despair. The former results from the belief that one always chooses the right and the good. Moral despair comes from the realization that we are fallible.

Through the character Judge William, Kierkegaard insists that moral decisions and actions be understood in terms of the dialectic of the temporal and the eternal. This means that, although the ethical self is unable to escape the aesthetic impulse to make choices that are for the satisfaction and fulfillment of bodily needs and social life, these choices are not given eternal validity. In the midst of a multiplicity of options, the individual has to find some higher good that affords constancy of self. The individual must "will one thing"—to surrender completely to the will of God.

So when all has become around one, as solemn as a starlit night, when the soul is alone in the whole world, then there appears before one, not a distinguished man, but the eternal Power itself. The heavens part, as it were, and the I chooses itself—or rather, receives itself. Then has the soul beheld the loftiest sight that the mortal eye can see and which never can be forgotten, then the personality receives the accolade of knighthood which enables it for an eternity. He does not become another man than he was before, but he becomes himself, consciousness is unified, and he is himself. As an heir, even were he heir to the treasure of all the world, nevertheless does not possess his property before he has come of age, so even the richest personality is nothing before he has chosen himself, and on the other hand even what one might call the poorest personality is everything when he has chosen himself; for the great thing is not to be this or that but to be oneself, and this everyone can be if he wills it.[27]

Kierkegaard therefore sublates aesthetic duty, that is, responsibility to the immediate-temporal demands of existence, to duty as an absolute ethical imperative to stand under the eternal governance of God. Divine guidance is necessary for such a choice. The existential demands of this choice are set forth in the religious sphere.

RELIGIOUS REPETITION: REPENTANCE AND FAITH

The young man in *Repetition* needs a religious repetition. Becoming a self before God is a continuing process of restoration in which the Christian chooses to repent and in so doing receives God's forgiveness. God alone brings about the wholeness of the self.

The Hebrew verb *subh* (to turn) is crucial for our understanding of repentance. The mutual turning of hearts by God and the people of God is dramatized in the formation of covenant. In the New Testament, this is expressed by the Greek verb *epistrephein,* to turn. The Vulgate uses the Latin verb *convertere.* Conversion is a dual process of repenting from sin and turning toward God. In the book of the Acts of the Apostles, Luke describes conversion as *metanoia*—a change of heart (Acts 3:19). Repentance is necessary for the forgiveness of sins (Acts 26:18-20).

Paul's conversion on the Damascus Road is generally considered a prototypical conversion. His visionary recognition of Christ is taken as evidence of a radical instantaneous transformation. There is, however, much debate whether Paul understood his experience of conversion as a matter of repentance and salvation, or whether his experience was a conversion in the popular sense of the term.

Krister Stendahl argues that Paul's experience "reveals a greater continuity between 'before and after,' " and that there is no "change of religion that we commonly associate with the word *conversion.*"[28] Stendahl places Paul's experience within the tradition of the prophets who were called to God's service.

Beverly Gaventa writes that Paul himself never describes a Damascus Road experience or applies the terms " 'turning' *(epistrophe)* or 'repentance' *(metanoia)* to himself"[29] and "never characterizes coming to faith as an act of repentance."[30] Citing II Corinthians 7:9-10, 12:21, and Romans 2:4, Gaventa points out that in every case Paul refers "to the repentance of persons who already possess faith in Jesus as Messiah."[31] She also finds Stendahl's "call" too narrow since it "does not encompass Paul's recognition of Jesus as Messiah or his radical change in values and commitments."[32] Furthermore, "The revelation of Jesus as Messiah brought about in Paul a transformed understanding of God and God's actions in the world."[33]

Gaventa defines transformation as

a radical change of perspective in which some newly gained cognition brings about a changed way of understanding. Unlike a conversion, a transformation does not require a rejection or negation of the past or of previously held values. Instead, a transformation involves a new perception, a re-cognition, of the past.[34]

It is a paradigm shift in the sense of Thomas Kuhn's analysis of scientific revolutions.[35] For Paul, this transformation revolved around the scandal of the Cross. The Messiah was not supposed to be present among a group of infidels and die as a common criminal on a cross, hence Paul's persecution of those of the Way. Citing evidence from Paul's letters and Luke-Acts (e.g., Gal. 1:16, Phil. 3:7-8, Acts 9:22, and Luke 26), Gaventa argues that the revelation of Jesus as the Son of God to Paul on the Damascus Road constituted a radical transformation from darkness to light.

Gaventa finds the moral aspects of Paul's transformation in the area of the messianic problem, but also makes a strong case for the religious dimension of this experience as the transformation of faith. Popular interest in Paul's conversion tends to focus only on the ecstatic experience as a moment of moral decision and proceeds to build proselytizing programs on this limited perspective. Paul himself made less of his Damascus Road experience and concentrated on God's initiative in calling persons to faith and the human response as a matter of faith. The pivotal event is not personal experience but God's revelation in Jesus on the cross at Calvary.

> The impact of this faith or confidence, which is granted by God, is to bring about not merely the conversion of believers but their transformation. Paul does not ask that people repent and turn around, but that they acknowledge God's new creation (Gal. 6:15; 2 Cor. 5:17) and allow themselves to be appropriated by it. Nowhere is this clearer than in Rom. 12:2: "Do not be conformed to this world, but be transformed by the renewal of your mind."[36]

The richness of Paul's conversion could occupy our undivided attention. This is not only beyond the scope of this study but also should be left to biblical scholars.[37] Suffice it to say,

Paul's conversion demonstrates that faith is God's gift of the impossible. Through faith, the impossible becomes possible. In Paul's case, the self is reborn in a radically new relationship with God. The recognition of the crucified Jesus as the Christ brings about a whole new form of self-understanding, indeed a new identity that is centered in a new community of faith, the body of Christ.

Paul's transformation is especially instructive to those who are overwhelmed by the uncertainty of the future, hence escape into the past, holding on to old ways of acting and old forms of self-understanding. Paul could escape neither his past nor God's call to new life. His response to God exemplifies what God expects of all who are called. His transformation was a decisive change from the law to gospel, from error to truth, from despair to faith, from darkness to light. In this transformation we see both continuity and discontinuity. The God of Saul the Jew is the God of Paul the Christian. The past is not denied or discarded but reinterpreted in light of the new relationship with God.

I contend that Paul's transformation concretely demonstrates what Kierkegaard means by repetition. Paul's life was retaken and redeemed by God and redirected toward a new way of being in the world. It brought about a new way of relating to the eternal—a life not free of personal suffering but in which personal suffering is outweighed by the happiness *(Salighed)* of eternal life. In the Kierkegaardian sense of repetition, Paul's transformation was not an end itself but the basis of a continual redefining of responsible selfhood. The Incarnation is given new meaning as the temporal is brought into a renewed relationship to the eternal. The earnestness of striving for this renewed selfhood is captured in Paul's second letter to the church at Corinth.

> So we do not lose heart. Even though our outer nature is wasting away, our inner nature is being renewed day by day. For this slight momentary affliction is preparing us for an eternal weight of glory beyond all measure, because we look not at what can be seen but at what cannot be seen; for what can be seen is temporary but what cannot be seen is eternal. (II Cor. 4:16-18)

TRANSFORMATION AND DISCIPLESHIP

It is not enough to testify to radical changes in one's relation to God without addressing the continuity of this relationship in Christian discipleship. Kierkegaard describes the divine-human relationship as one between a disciple (one who does not possess the truth) and the Teacher (one who possesses the truth). The Teacher not only provides the disciple with the truth but with the condition for discovering the truth—that the disciple may become "a person for a different quality . . . a *new* person."[38]

This movement from untruth to truth, Kierkegaard defines as conversion. It involves repentance—the awareness of fault and the sorrow of being embedded in a state of untruth. Repentance is looking back at one's former state while at the same time looking forward to what lies ahead. The transition from untruth to truth is existentially a transition from nonbeing to being. In actuality, this is "the transition of birth."[39] Since birth has already occurred, the transition from nonbeing to being is "rebirth."

> Just as the person who by Socratic midwifery gave birth himself and in so doing forgot everything else in the world and in a more profound sense owed no human being anything, so also the one who is born again owes no human being anything, but owes the divine teacher everything. And just as the other one, because of himself, forgot the whole world, so he in turn, because of this teacher, must forget himself.[40]

Socrates is not the divine Teacher. His disciples owed him nothing. Socrates assisted his disciples in coming into existence only indirectly by the *maieutic* art of indirect communication. In contrast, the transformation of selfhood is the direct action of the divine Teacher. The disciple is born anew and owes this new life to the Teacher. He or she who would be a disciple must be willing to surrender his or her life for the sake of this love. The authenticity of the self is constituted only when the self rests transparently in God. "I am myself again" is an affirmation that the self is once again redeemed by God.

CONTEMPORANEITY WITH CHRIST

In a tinsel society where the external *persona* is the totality of selfhood, faith is easily collapsed into the fulfillment of wishes and the satisfaction of desires. Puncturing these cultural masks reveals the utter shallowness of our lives. Sometimes it takes a tragedy to catapult us out of this sphere of existence.

Today, we are faced with the collective shallowness of a narcotic existence. Drug addiction has created a collective "psychic numbing," a modern leveling process from which there seems to be no enduring emancipation. As in Kierkegaard's *"symparanekromenoi"* or "fellowship of buried lives," some of us are living as though we were dead.[41] It seems as though we are not only in the last decade of the twentieth century but in the last throes of human existence.

Given the negative forces of existence, it is easy to escape into a rigid moralism in order to find unambiguous distinctions between good and evil, and between right and wrong. We want to be assured that we are always on God's side. We conflate moral rectitude and religious piety. Yet, we live in moral despair. Our fallibility militates against the eternal security of moral choices and faithfulness to God. For the Christian, striving to do God's will is especially troublesome.

Kierkegaard therefore moves the discussion of the moral life and religious faith into the realm of becoming Christian. Whereas the Kantian moral self rests on the practice of moral reason, Kierkegaard teleologically suspends the ethical, liberates it from the categories of universal moral reason, and connects it directly to the passion of Jesus Christ. Moral reasoning is sublated to faith in Christ. For Kierkegaard the Lutheran, the Christian is justified by faith alone. The striving for eternal salvation is to be understood paradoxically as a striving with "fear and trembling" and a "leap of faith." This "paradox of intention"[42] is a "paradox of grace"—the despair of seeking the eternal and the willingness to accept the eternal as a gift of God.

In the medieval tradition of the *imitatio Christi*, Kierkegaard found a noble example of Christian discipleship. This tradition emulated the earnestness and discipline of becoming Christian.

A significant problem with this life-style was its understanding of history. These disciplines were attempts to authenticate Christian faith on some pristine way of being in the world. Kierkegaard approaches the problem of recovering the relation to Christ in a very different way. Christian faith is not authenticated by efforts to enter into the time and person of Jesus Christ. On the contrary, the enduring task of discipleship is to become *contemporaneous* with Christ. This does not mean retreating into the past in order to retrieve some pristine experience of Jesus Christ.

Christian faith rests on the Incarnation. Through the Incarnation, time has been retaken by God. The Christian vocation is to re-present the Incarnation in the world believing that the temporal has already been transformed by Christ even as we anticipate his coming again. Witnessing to Christ's presence in our time means finding ways to make the love of Christ work in the world. This is done through our love of neighbor. Every act of love becomes part of the God-relationship. In other words, love of neighbor repeats the presence of the eternal in time. God bestows eternal meaning on our efforts to love as God loves.

Here the distinction between ethical religion (Religiousness A or the religion of immanence) and Christian faith (Religiousness B or paradoxical religiousness) is crucial. Religiousness A is marked by the relativization of the finite, which occurs when the individual experiences moral despair—the realization that the authenticity of the self is constantly undermined by the inability to perform all the moral duties with which the self is confronted. The self surrenders to God. In so doing, the demands of finitude are made relative.

The aesthetic self, living in the religion of immanence, "finds no contradiction in the fact of existing: to exist is one thing, and the contradiction is something else that comes from without. *The ethical* finds the contradiction, but within self-assertion."[43] Stated differently, the aesthetic self progresses along life's way in a series of rotations, stimulated by the eternal possibility of discovering meaning within the temporal. The ethical self realizes that the resolutions of the moral life are not eternal. The temporal-eternal conflict persists. Empowered by reason, the ethical self lives triumphantly with Religiousness A.

Religiousness A is a prerequisite of Christian faith (Religiousness B). Religiousness A is a kind of natural religion in that it begins with the immanence of the self, then expands into a natural consciousness of the eternal. Its transformative character is a kind of repentance by which the individual "repents himself back into himself, back into the family, into the race, until he finds himself in God." Becoming a self before God, that is, being measured by the absolute standard of the relation to God, is an exhaustive detour through finitude. God is located within a system of relations in which faith is defined by the self's interaction with finitude and with God. This resonates with what we have seen in James' practical theism and Fowler's stages of faith. Not surprisingly, this type of religiousness is exemplified by Kierkegaard's pseudonym Climacus, the climber. A Christian view of the relation to God is given by Anti-Climacus.[44]

The whole point of Christianity (paradoxical religiousness) is that it is a repetition of the Incarnation—"an absurd coincidence of opposites which unyieldingly resists all rational, historical, and religious mediation."[45] The Christian either believes this or is offended. Authentic Christian selfhood begins when a person chooses as his or her single purpose in life the task of witnessing to the truth of the Incarnation. This means that one is willing to live with the paradoxes of crucifixion and resurrection, suffering and hope. The aesthete evades the demands of this radical life and chooses instead the easy life of transforming finite satisfactions into an illusory eternal fulfillment.

The ethical individual strives to actualize a creative ethical synthesis of body and soul by appealing to universal principles of the right and the good. If there is a lesson to be learnt from Abraham's relation to God, it is that God does demand of the righteous more than what fits universal or deontological principles of the right and the good. Kierkegaard refuses to sublate the religious to the ethical. The ethical is anchored in the relationship to God and not the other way around. By becoming human in Jesus Christ, God participates in our quest for authenticity. Were this simply an ethical posture, we would not need Jesus Christ. For Kierkegaard, it is only in relation to Christ that the awareness of sin is most fully realized and the spiritual synthesis of body and soul actualized. Neither the aesthete's guilt over the inability to find an eternally meaningful experience, nor the ethical individual's guilt over the inability to maintain eternal righteousness is equivalent to the sin that comes from the refusal to choose to become a self before God. For Christians, this means choosing to be like Christ, to *re-present* Christ in our time. To re-present Christ in our time is to believe that Christ forgives our sins and offers us new life. It is to live with the "objective uncertainty" of faith.

The passion *(Lidenskab)* of faith is the existential repetition of the suffering *(Lidende)* of the God-Man. It is the imitatio Christi that gives birth to spirit. The wayfarer at last joins the young man portrayed in *Repetition* to declare: "I am born to myself." But the moment always passes. The genuine coincidence of opposites within the self is only momentary, and must be repeatedly reconstituted. The existing individual never *is* spirit; rather he *becomes* spirit. The self's spiritual birth is a labor of a lifetime. The final enjoyment of the fruits of this lifelong labor is eschatological.[46]

Part of the profundity of Christian faith is the resolve to live as if our time is the end of time. The Incarnation stands as a moment in time when the human is reborn to the eternal Power that permeates all of existence. One either believes this or is offended. The self that is unable to grasp a moment in time when it is reborn to the Power which constituted it is without an eternal anchor for relating to the future. Straddled between an elusive past and an unactualized future, the self becomes Kierkegaard's "Unhappiest Man."[47]

Living contemporaneously with the "God-man" means living with the offense of the cross and the promise of new life in Christ. This calls for a leap of faith—an existential "breach with immanence."[48] This begins with passionate self-examination. We deceive ourselves if this examination does not lay bare before us the ontological fragmentation of the self into body and soul, and the "spiritlessness" that ensues from this misrelation to God. To will to live in this state of despair is sin. For Kierkegaard, sin is the opposite of faith. It is to reject the opportunity for authentic selfhood.

Passionate self-examination yields repentance and forgiveness of sin. For the Christian, this is not enough. To live contemporaneously with the crucified and resurrected Christ is to take on the suffering of one's neighbor. In the present age, the demands of loving one's neighbor are overwhelming. Solidarity with victims means courageously responding to the tragedies of AIDS, drug addiction, homelessness and poverty, and countless other conditions that seem unchangeable and hopeless. Living contemporaneously with Christ is a continual praxis of *metanoia* of self and world. Kierkegaard does not isolate the individual from the rest of the world. On the contrary, he rejects any form of "monkish" retreat from the world or philosophical abstraction of the individual from existence. Becoming a self before God is impossible without love of neighbor.

To conclude this discussion, becoming a self before God means becoming free to love God and to help others and ourselves love God as neighbor. For the Christian, this means living contemporaneously with Christ. The self that is authentically reborn through faith in the crucified and resurrected Christ does not hide behind the past, especially past accomplishments or doctrines, which prevent the individual from being decisive in recommitting himself or herself to bringing the temporal into the God-relationship.

The radical paradox of the Incarnation places Christ fully in our time and yet not in our time. The Incarnation is a beacon for illumining the past. Because of the Incarnation, the guilt-consciousness of the past is met by forgiveness and restoration. The Incarnation is a plumb line for evaluating our decisiveness in choosing the highest ethical good with which authentic selfhood is identified, namely, eternal happiness *(Salighed)*. The Incarnation crystallizes for the Christian the arduous yet blessed task of religious repetition—the transformation of existence by bringing the temporal into our relationship to God. This is the matrix from which we bear our losses, disappointments, and tragedies. Religious repetition is a recasting of these events in the light of the enduring presence of God in time. Without religious repetition, Christian faith degenerates into a static and imperious religion, an oppressive Christendom characterized by its resistance to change and its failure to re-present the love of Christ in our time.

CHAPTER SIX

KENOTIC
TRANSFORMATIONS

If anyone is in Christ, [that person] is a new creation.

—II Corinthians 5:17

The Christian life begins in transformation.

—Richard Bondi, *Leading God's People*[1]

In this chapter, we examine the dialectic of formation and imitation in Christian discipleship from the perspective of kenotic christology.

The nineteenth century marked a watershed in the history of Protestant theology. Schleiermacher's *magnum opus, The Christian Faith,* revolutionized the interpretation of the divine-human relationship by shifting the center of gravity from the transcendence of the *Logos* to the experience of the human Christ in the world. The stage was set for a humanistic thrust in modern christology. Writing two decades after Schleiermacher, Gottfried Thomasius offered his own distinctive contribution to the christological debate.[2] Thomasius' ideas reflect Hegel's influence on much of nineteenth-century philosophical and theological thought.

Thomasius argued that the christological problem pivoted on the voluntary self-limitation of the divine Logos in the incarnate Son, Jesus Christ. Thomasius disagreed with Schleiermacher's argument that the Incarnation marked the fulfillment of God's creation of humanity. For one thing, this argument vitiated the mystery of the Incarnation—a position carried to the extreme by Feuerbach in his argument that God is simply a projection of the human mind and Christ a representation of the divinity that is present in all of humanity.

In order to preserve the traditional distinction between the divine and the human, Thomasius argued that a distinctive feature of God's love is God's self-limitation. The christological problem was not to determine whether Christ was fully divine and fully human at the same time but whether the life, suffering, and death of Jesus Christ was indeed the enactment of God's love for humanity. The key issue for Thomasius was God's freedom to limit God's self in loving humanity. The *kenosis* of Jesus Christ was not merely the surrender of divine power but the Incarnation of divine love. Here we see the continuity between the self-emptying of God (the *Logos asarkos*) in the Incarnation and the humiliation of Jesus Christ (the *Logos ensarkos*).

In arguing for divine self-limitation, Thomasius also distinguished between the immanent attributes of God, for example, God's love, truth, absolute power, and holiness, and relative attributes such as omnipotence, omnipresence, and omniscience. The latter were given up in the Incarnation.[3] According to Lucien Richard, "Thomasius' insistence on the reality of the divine self-emptying challenged the traditional teaching on the immutability and impassibility of God."[4] Moreover, in diminishing the essence or substance of the Incarnation of God in the person of Jesus, Thomasius assaulted traditional Trinitarian theology, thereby finding favor with the Hegelians who "accepted the changes and limitations demanded by kenosis as a necessary stage in the development of the Absolute."[5] The Hegelian elements in Thomasius' christology require further explication.

Thomasius interpreted the God-Jesus relationship in terms of Hegelian Idealism as the development of self-consciousness. This development begins with the Incarnation. In that act, self-consciousness is already given in potency, but at first only in the form of pure immediacy into which the divine-human ego is surrendered. From this condition it works itself out gradually.

As consciousness concerning his innermost nature arises for the growing and developing child Jesus, there opens up for him at the same time the consciousness of his sonship to God, of his relationship to the Father, and of his vocation as the Redeemer of the world, just as for us, in the course of the natural spiritual unfolding of life, consciousness concerning kinship to God and our earthly destiny takes its rise with self-consciousness.[6]

This developmental scheme has the essential elements of Hegelian dialectical diachronic development. Self-limitation and humiliation are dialectically related in the maturing Jesus, mediated by the Holy Spirit. In other words, the full humanity of Christ is interpreted as a developmental progression in which the dialectic of self-fulfillment *(plerosis)* and self-emptying *(kenosis)* is mediated by the Holy Spirit.

Macquarrie chides Thomasius for being "too cautious in asserting the full humanity of Christ."[7] Citing Pannenberg, he suggests that the Incarnation has "a mythological tone."[8] Hence, methodologically, the starting point should not be the Incarnation but the crucified and risen Lord. Contrary to the Hegelianism in Thomasius' christology, Macquarrie argues that

the idea of *kenosis* acquires a new relevance and a fuller meaning when we begin with the humiliation of Christ in his earthly and human life, with the self-abasement of the human Jesus as he goes obediently to the cross. For it is this utter self-outpouring that constitutes his glory and that transfigures him so that God-language becomes a necessity if we are to speak of him with any adequacy. The paradox is that his abasement is also his exultation.[9]

Macquarrie underscores the paradox of *kenosis*.

This is the paradox of personal existence, that emptying and fulfilling, *kenosis* and *plerosis* are the same; and he who utterly emptied himself, Jesus Christ, is precisely the one who permits us to glimpse that utter fulness that we call divine.

It is only in the light of the human self-emptying of Jesus Christ that we can venture to speak of a self-emptying of the eternal Logos as a clue to the meaning of incarnation.[10]

Macquarrie adheres to Kierkegaard's notion of the Incarnation as the Absolute Paradox. *Kenosis* is diminished if the humanity of Christ is separated from his divinity. The *kenosis* of Christ is both the unique sacrifice of the man Jesus for the sake of humanity and the revelation of God as eternally self-emptying, self-limiting, and self-giving.

In challenging Hegelian historicism, Kierkegaard demonstrated that the Christian could not rest the task of becoming Christian on the process of history, however sacred some historical events were to the formation of Christian identity. Christianity rests on the Absolute Paradox of the Incarnation. The Christian ethico-religious response to this event is to make Christ present in our time. We have seen this in Kierkegaard's concept of contemporaneity with Christ.

Obviously, we cannot re-enter the time zone of the historical Jesus. But we can respond to Jesus' invitation to enter into his humiliation. According to Kierkegaard, it was not from his glory but from his humiliation that Jesus extended his invitation: "Come to me, all who labor and are heavy laden, and I will give you rest" (Matt. 11:28 RSV).

In choosing the way of the cross, Jesus concretely established his solidarity with victims, thereby making solidarity with victims the locus for a self-critical understanding of contemporaneity with Christ, and, as Matthew Lamb observes, "an imperative for responsible theology today."[11] For Lamb, becoming Christian is inevitably a journey of intensification into the history of suffering. Suffering is an irruption of history. It is the locus where contemporaneity with Christ meets its greatest challenge. Lamb is therefore correct in directing our attention to the self-critical task of bearing the burden of others as they seek to become authentic selves before God. This project between self and other is ethically mandated in the commandment to love one's neighbor as oneself. The corrective to exploitative self-love is love of neighbor. Love of neighbor is a necessary condition for my own authenticity. In the language of liberation theology, we could say that becoming Christian means a prior recognition of the other as my neighbor—one who is engaged in the task of authenticating selfhood the same as I am and whose liberation from oppression is the condition for my own liberation.

Taking Kierkegaard's forms of despair as analogous to forms of oppression, I suggest that the quest for authentic selfhood is a spiritual journey that involves raising to consciousness the unconscious forms of oppression that are buried deep within cultural norms of human behavior. This kind of oppression is similar to what Kierkegaard calls "despair *in* weakness."[12] Such oppression allows persons to perpetuate structures of injustice without perceiving their complicity. At the opposite extreme is defiant despair, which refuses to acknowledge its guilt. This is exemplified by megalomaniacal bigots who defiantly will to perpetuate conditions of oppression.

Then there is the "despair *of* weakness." This is the inability to move beyond the state of oppression. During the sixties, I attended many conferences on racial justice in which some of my colleagues would confess their inability to create any significant transformation of their existence. Like the characters in Becket's *Waiting for Godot,* they were waiting for some dramatic event to transform history, meanwhile fearing too sudden a change. Both black and white liberals agonized that militant blacks were about to bring about a bloody revolution. In his *Pedagogy of the Oppressed,* Paulo Freire describes a similar form of consciousness.[13] Existing in the despair of weakness, the oppressed take on the worst characteristics of their oppressors. They become their worst oppressors, unable to bring about any meaningful liberation in their lives.

Kierkegaard's metaphor of contemporaneity with Christ prompts an examination of the forms of despair that impede our ability to respond to the suffering of the world. Contemporaneity with Christ has both moral and religious imperatives. Morally, it requires that we assume responsibility for liberating ourselves and others from social and political structures of oppression. The religious imperative is to enact the image of Christ in our lives and in our relationships. In the effort to alleviate or eliminate oppression, it is easy to settle for the religion of immanence ("Religiousness A"). Alienation from God is endured and we courageously will to do the right and the good. The problem is that we remain entombed in the despair *of*

111

weakness—the moral despair of being unable to eliminate suffering by consistent acts of goodness. Christianity, "Religiousness B," offers a radical approach to the problem of suffering. It invites disciples to be baptized into the suffering, death, and resurrection of Jesus Christ. This is not an individual experience. The Christian is baptized into a community of faith. Through the metaphor of the body of Christ, Paul exhorts Christians to see themselves through the lives of the least among us—those at risk in the barrios, refugee camps, reservations, and ghettos; the homeless, and those in the "homelands" of South Africa; the marginal of the world wherever they are. In this venture we are illumined by the self-emptying of Christ. In summary, contemporaneity with Christ involves a *theologia crucis* in which the *kenosis* of Christ is the paradigm of Christian formation and imitation.

THE PARADOX OF GRACE

A kenotic spirituality embraces the paradox of resoluteness in Christian discipleship. In this paradox, the will seeks decisiveness and fulfillment; spirit invites the surrender of self to the transforming power of God. The surrender of self does not compromise freedom of will or undermine ethical decisiveness. The disciple must choose to surrender to Christ but, as Paul reminds us in Romans 7, the will does not bring about the changes desired. "I can will what is right, but I cannot do it. For I do not do the good I want, but the evil I do not want is what I do" (RSV). Will is saved only by the grace of God.

We learn from the spiritual journeys of mystics such as Teresa of Avila, John of the Cross, and Meister Eckhart that the issues of ultimate meaning and belonging call for a spirituality of will and spirit, contemplation and action, questing and waiting, fulfillment and self-emptying. This faithful imagination allows us to become fully immersed in loving God and our neighbor without fear of being overcome by despair. Through God's self-emptying love, humanity comes fully into existence.

Using Kierkegaard's terminology, we could say that the *kenosis* of Christ is a *repetition (Gjentagelsen)*. It takes up again the Incarnation in a new way. The "fullness of time" is paradoxically the self-emptying of Christ. This is a redemptive act. Once again God overcomes the distance of history. The human is given over fully to God and God to the human in the suffering of Christ. Christians are called to imaginatively re-create, through works of love, God's self-emptying love. What God has done in Christ becomes for the disciple a fresh opportunity for participating in the liberation of humanity.

The passion or pain of God is taken up again in the humiliation of Jesus Christ, and the humiliation of Christ is forever embraced by God as the decisive mark of Christ's humanity. For the Christian, the *kenosis* of Christ is an opportunity for the leap of faith and thus an occasion for offense. The "absolutely paradoxical passion of faith" is not a matter to be logically explicated.[14] It is to be *performed* each time the believer participates in the humiliation of Christ by bearing the suffering of humanity. In so doing the believer lives contemporaneously with Christ. The *kenosis* of Christ crystallizes what is already a fact of existence—self-emptying and self-fulfillment—without transmuting one into the other.

Douglas John Hall echoes these Kierkegaardian sentiments in his insistence that a kenotic theology of the Cross *(theologia crucis)* is necessary for understanding the hard paradoxes of becoming Christian.[15] Unfortunately, we live in a culture that has little tolerance for paradox of any kind, especially one that involves suffering and negation. A theology of glory *(theologia gloriae)* fits comfortably into a triumphalist culture.

THE PAIN OF GOD

We have reached a watershed in history when we must re-image the Incarnation in the light of God's compassion, literally, God's "suffering with" humanity. Paul's rendition of the Crucifixion as the *kenosis* of Christ recapitulates the pain of God established in the Incarnation. I adapt the phrase "pain of God" from Kazoh Kitamori's seminal work on the subject. "The theology of the pain of God," writes Kitamori, "does not mean that pain exists in God as *substance*. The pain of God is not a 'concept of substance'—it is a 'concept of relation,' a nature of

'God's love.' "[16] Stated differently, the "pain of God" refers to God's suffering with humanity.

The similarity with Kierkegaard's notion of the passion of God is striking. The passion of God is God's willingness to enter into a loving relationship with humanity, concretely in the Incarnation, and to dramatize this relationship in the *kenosis* of Christ. The *kenosis* of Christ is ultimately a horizon for understanding the meaning of the Incarnation and the meaning of authentic selfhood. With the *kenosis* of Christ, God's being-in-time (God's suffering with humanity) is performed as if it were for the first time—an utterly true and authentic repetition. The *kenosis* of Christ negates the question of the impassibility of God (God's exemption from suffering) and accentuates the transfiguration of human suffering by God's suffering with humanity. It is on this basis that we are confident in God's solidarity with the marginal of the world.

Moved by the pathos of social and political injustice, liberation and political theologians proclaim the "preferential option of the poor" or the epistemological privilege of the oppressed.[17] The actual and particular condition of poverty or suffering is taken as the locus for establishing the truth and authenticity of God's emancipatory praxis. Here, God's incarnate presence is revealed and human selfhood authenticated by God's self-emptying. Liberation theologians eschew the idealization or spiritualization of suffering. They do not subscribe to its rationalization as a necessary experience for cultivating moral character or faith.

Process theologian Delwin Brown chides liberation theologians for ignoring important metaphysical assumptions about God's emancipatory praxis. Brown disputes the "hermeneutic judgment" of liberation theologians that "liberation" is the "semantic axis" of the Bible. He argues that "the claim that the liberationist message is the biblical message is not privileged, at least not in the sense that the judgment in its favor somehow escapes being assessed as the projection of a particular, interest-laden grid."[18] His main point is that there is no singular social location or biblical perspective from which the authenticity of the biblical message is determined. Thus he is critical of the failure of liberation theologians to justify and substantiate the claim of "epistemological privilege" held by the poor. Brown proposes, instead, the "epistemological priority" of the poor. By this he means that "all Christian claims to truth must be tested in relationship to the experience of the poor, just as they are subject to scrutiny in terms of every human perspective."[19]

To see the experience of the poor, therefore, as one among several possible perspectives from which to evaluate the truth claims of the gospel, does not explain the "epistemological priority of the poor." Though he sees this as a primary "obligation," Brown offers no moral justification. In typical process thought he appeals to a metaphysical framework in which reality is dynamic and relational.

> On this analysis, "solidarity with the poor and the oppressed" would not be an obligation based on some form of Christian special pleading: in enunciating this obligation the Christian would merely be articulating an obligation made evident by any adequate analysis of what knowing means and how, in fact, human beings have known historically.[20]

Brown is critical of epistemological absolutism. His metaphysical stance begins with the concrete perspective but moves toward developing "a general scheme of concepts or ideas in terms of which all else may be adequately interpreted and consistently explicated."[21] This logic requires that the concrete situation that sets forth claims of its priority ought to be the setting in which the truth of these claims is first tested. The truth of the claim that the poor enjoy an epistemological priority is to be tested first in the situation of oppression. Moreover, "Every claim about God must be examined in the scathing light of experienced oppression, there, if anywhere, to be stipulated as adequate and acceptable."[22]

Practically speaking, the epistemological priority of the poor means that critical dialogue on God's emancipatory praxis *ought to* include the poor. The argument for the "preferential option of the poor" essentially calls attention to the *locus* of suffering as the point of reference for the authentication of selfhood. This is precisely why the *kenosis* of Christ is not a recollection but a repetition. It is repeated each time and every time we empty ourselves in love for the liberation of humanity. Brown's argument for the epistemological priority of the poor rests on a philosophical stance regarding the particularity and relativity of human experience. Given his rejection of a common human experience (except our ability to communicate with one another), he is forced to rely on multiperspectival conversations about truth claims, including the claims of the Incarnation and *kenosis*. In keeping with the pragmatist-process philosophical tradition, truth is established by way of its coherence with other truths. Brown points out that "it is difficult to see how ideas can be sustained in practice over the long haul if they are not coherent and consistent with the other things we believe to be true and therefore act upon."[23] The truth and value of the epistemological priority of the poor are realized in the coherence and consistency of this claim with other claims of God's liberating and salvific action. In other words, the epistemological priority of the poor calls for a critical evaluation of the problem of suffering.

H. Richard Niebuhr, whose close connection with pragmatism and process thought has already been mentioned, points out the methodological deficiencies of teleological and deontological ethics in addressing the problem of suffering. Teleological ethics has to do with the purposes and consequences of action. Deontological ethics is concerned with duties and obligations. Neither addresses adequately the subversiveness and irruption of suffering in human existence; hence, suffering calls for an ethics of responsibility. Within this framework, suffering is neither an objective to be overcome nor a phenomenon that operates according to external rules or laws, but is a condition in which we are acted upon and one that evokes responsible action.

According to Niebuhr's ethic of responsibility, the truth claims of the suffering do not end with those who suffer, but fit into a wider, continuing, value-creating process in which the nonsuffering are included. Unlike Brown, Niebuhr does not shy away from absolutes. There is an overarching "whole," namely, the kingdom of God, in which all of humanity is included. Brown, on the other hand, maintains an open-ended value-creating process in which the locus of the poor is the

appropriate circumstance for formulating theologies of liberation for the poor and those not poor. In this process, Brown
wants critical reflection on praxis in liberation theology to
include metaphysical considerations. The latter are defined as
"the tentative effort to seek coherence and consistency, the
perspectival effort to seek relevant generality."[24] Brown's
objective is not to legitimate liberation on the basis of some
neo-Cartesian exercise in cerebral gymnastics, but to expand the
perimeters of theological discourse so that the liberation of the
oppressed may be consistent and coherent with the entirety of
the divine-human relationship.

As a process theologian, Brown limits transformation to the
perpetuation of establishing continuity between the liberation
of the oppressed and the pluralistic environment in which
religious beliefs are located. In the final analysis, suffering is not
viewed as an irruption of history but as a part of the continuing
historical transformation of creation. There is an underlying
assumption that God and humanity are working together in
perfecting creation. This theistic humanism does not attribute
any uniqueness to the Incarnation or the *kenosis* of Christ. These
events belong to immanent time and may be recollected as part
of the self's subjective existence. It is not surprising then that
John Cobb, one of America's preeminent process theologians,
sees himself in such close agreement with Johannes Metz's
narrative hermeneutic of faith in history.[25] Both Cobb and Metz
place the emancipatory praxis of theology on the remembrance
of suffering and the power of such "dangerous memories" to
bring about moral and religious transformational response to
these narratives.

A spirituality of suffering that considers the Incarnation and
the *kenosis* of Christ as events to be recollected into autobiogra-
phy has the same pitfalls as psychologies that place the burden
of human liberation on the remembrance of the past.
Remembrance in and of itself is not liberating. Self-deception
leads to the creation of illusory beginnings and endings.

Remembrance alone offers no cure. Nor does it offer religious
salvation. Persistent memories of past evil, suffered or perpe-
trated, far from being redemptive have gradually drained the
faith from many a believer's heart.[26]

117

Critics of liberation theology are quick to note its appropriation of historicism, especially Marxist historical materialism. A principal contribution of kenotic christology is that it sets forth a basis for the paradoxical overcoming of the distance of history—not by recollection but by repetition. The humiliation of Christ becomes the point of contact between the sacred event on the cross and the suffering of humanity in the world today. By taking on the suffering of the neighbor, the Christian becomes a contemporary of Christ. This repetition is neither a regression to the historical event (which would be impossible) nor a projection into a future from some idealized point in the present (which would be illusory).

A kenotic spirituality of suffering revolves around the act of being entirely present to oneself. To be entirely present to oneself is to empty oneself of every claim to selfhood. It is to recognize that I am not what I ought to be, namely, to live as a person who is being formed in the likeness of Christ. In a word, it is to acknowledge my sinfulness. Only then is genuine transformation possible—in the form of forgiveness. If this is not the transcendent principle that transforms our relation to one another and to God, what is?

Advocates of liberation and political theologies are hard pressed to speak about repentance and forgiveness as actions that are incumbent on the oppressed and the oppressors. Caught in the religion of immanence, issues of social justice and freedom are robbed of transcendence. To dare bring the humiliation of Christ into center stage may easily be construed as an attempt to reinforce stereotypes of the subservient slave whose liberation will come only by remaining meek and mild. But this is a terrible caricature of kenotic spirituality. The humiliation of Christ is inherently paradoxical. Any of us who dares to live contemporaneously with Christ will have to face the fact that this undertaking is not about being humble in response to oppressive power but is about taking on the pain of God in the world. In the *kenosis* of Christ, God becomes one with human pain, but this immanence is met paradoxically by God's transcendent love through which human pain is embraced and sin forgiven. Kitamori is therefore correct in declaring that the "pain of God" is not a substance ontology that has to do with God's independent being. On the contrary, it has to do with God's self-emptying love—God's choice in freedom to take on the pathos of human existence.[27] The hardest part of living contemporaneously with Christ is to let God's self-emptying love in Christ become for us a way of loving God and one another.

CHAPTER SEVEN

LETTING GO,
RISKING CHRIST

Let the same mind be in you that was in
Christ Jesus,
who, though he was in the form of God,
    did not regard equality with God
    as something to be exploited,
but emptied himself,
    taking the form of a slave,
    being born in human likeness,
And being found in human form,
    he humbled himself
    and became obedient to the point of death—
    even death on a cross.
Therefore God also highly exalted him
    and gave him the name
    that is above every name,
so that at the name of Jesus
    every knee should bend,
    in heaven and on earth and
        under the earth,
and every tongue should confess
    that Jesus Christ is Lord,
    to the glory of God the Father.

—Philippians 2:5-11

Only he who has dared to let go can dare to re-enter.

—Meister Eckhart[1]

In this concluding chapter, I would like to reflect on the implications of the kenotic christology for the transformation of the Church. At the outset, I must admit that my understanding of what the Church is and what it does has been shaped by Anglicanism, particularly its balancing of scripture, reason, tradition, and experience in forging a middle path *(via media)* in moral theology and doctrine. This posture epitomizes dialectic and paradox in that it is dynamic and flexible, allowing for change and growth without losing fundamental values and beliefs.[2]

The genius of the *via media* is its ability to contain the hard paradoxes of Christian faith and the moral life in the practice of liturgy. Liturgy expresses a fundamental dialectic of theory and praxis in Anglicanism, according to which theology is shaped by liturgical praxis even as praxis is shaped by theology. In other words, the *via media* fosters consensus and is open to continual revision. The Anglican theologian W. Taylor Stevenson notes that the first Prayer Book of 1549, some three centuries later than the *Magna Carta,* exhibits significant parallels to the process of revision and consensus that produced the *Magna Carta.*[3] He suggests that the same spirit of revision continues in modern Anglicanism. That this is so is largely due to the prevalence of a contractarian ethic, which promotes order, stability, reasonableness, and unity. But Stevenson also admits that pragmatism and the desire for unity can degenerate into compromises that undermine the prophetic imagination and the evangelical ministry of the Anglican Church.

In addressing the problem of fostering change, growth, and development in the Anglican Church, Stevenson draws on Ricoeur's dialectical hermeneutic of retrieval and suspicion to interpret liturgical renewal in the Anglican Church.[4] A "hermeneutics of retrieval" enriches our present interpretation of the world by recovering and renewing the deeper traditions upon which our interpretation is founded. It presupposes that out of this retrieval will emerge new and imaginative forms of understanding. A "hermeneutics of suspicion" discloses the latent meanings or ideologies underlying our interpretation of the world. Retrieval reshapes understanding of the world by

121

expanding the horizon of meaning. Suspicion re-orders our understanding by illumining our distortions and illusions.

Stevenson alludes to the problem of generating change in an institution that resists absolutes and tries to preserve continuity in its identity through liturgy. He laments the loss of identity and creativity in twentieth-century Anglican theology and recommends that the way ahead for Anglican theology "is not through some revolutionary new beginning but rather through a reappropriation of its lost vision of the centrality of *lex orandi, lex credendi* in the life and thought of the Church."[5] He therefore urges Anglicans to recover the dialectical process by which symbols give rise to new meanings that evoke critical reflection on the symbols, which in turn gives rise to new thoughts. Stevenson sees this dialectical process as "eschatologically oriented toward the new, the future. All claims to finality and completion fall under the rubric of suspicion and the process continues."[6]

I do not dispute Stevenson's point that moral and spiritual renewal in the Anglican Church is inseparable from its liturgical life. My concern is that cultural pluralism be recognized as a normative feature of the Church. A hermeneutic of suspicion and retrieval helps to re-vision the pluralistic identity of the Church in light of its history and to discern the distortions of the truth in its history. But there is something missing in this hermeneutic, namely, an emancipatory praxis for widening the horizons of the Church's identity as it responds to the moral and theological imperatives of a culturally pluralistic world. This point is addressed by Thomas Ogletree in his "hermeneutics of hospitality."[7]

The point of a hermeneutics of hospitality is "to welcome strange and unfamiliar meanings into our own awareness, perhaps to be shaken by them, but in no case to be left unchanged. These meanings enable us to become aware of limitations in the concrete historicity of our own view of things."[8] This is a difficult task for the Anglican Church, given its complicity in imperialism and colonialism. A hermeneutics of hospitality raises the question of who is included in the contractarian ethic of Anglicanism. Surely, the days of "reasonable men" deciding who is to be included in the Anglican Church are about to pass into history. Moreover, the very nature of the Church as a communion of communions calls for an ethic of inclusiveness other than the ethic of contractarianism.

Under the critical lenses of a hermeneutics of hospitality, the emancipatory praxis of the Church is brought to the forefront of the Church's identity. It discloses that the Anglican communion cannot ignore the narratives of Christians from the underside of history—Africa, Asia, the South Pacific, Latin America, and the Caribbean—whose stories of the humiliated Christ among the poor and oppressed of the world have charted new forms of theological reflection and action. Now the whole Church is vulnerable to being changed by the testimonies and narratives of Christians whose faith in Christ has been shaped by the conditions of marginality.

FORMING NEW COVENANTS

The question then is whether the heritage of the *via media* can withstand the tests of inclusiveness and pluralism brought by women and other strangers from the underside of history. Their experiences deserve center stage in modern Anglicanism. Thanks to liberation theologians, the emancipatory praxis of the gospel is being elevated as the fulcrum of Scripture. The moral matrix of tradition is being called into question. Feudalism, patriarchy, and colonialism can no longer be ignored. Reason, a beacon of Anglican sensibility in a morally ambiguous and pluralistic world, now has to include a critique of domination, without which its comprehensiveness is seriously compromised.

Not all the constituencies of the Anglican Communion have been affected by the winds of change. Neo-colonialists ignore the narratives of emancipation and the dangerous memories of those who bear the scars of colonialism. They see the Anglican Communion as the sixteenth-century Church of England exported to various parts of the world. In a neo-colonialist situation, a hermeneutics of hospitality requires that both the colonized and the colonizers let go of the distortions and prejudices of the colonial life-world, which estrange people from themselves. A genuine moral transformation occurs when the alienated self is recognized and brought into the conversation between the colonized and colonizers.

The contemporary global situation calls for new forms of covenantal living that will sustain the interdependence of the peoples of the world, and our responsibility for preserving the ecosystem. William May identifies three principal components of covenant: (1) the experience of the relationship as a gift shared by partners; (2) an exchange of promises, for example, the Ten Commandments; (3) the subsequent restructuring of life in response to the promissory event.[9] To be in covenant with God is to respond to the One who first called humanity into relationship and whose faithfulness is the measure of our own. The covenantal relationship sustains repentance and forgiveness. Scripture is replete with narratives of God and the people of God turning away from and returning to each other.

The Anglican Communion has evolved as a communion of communions in which no single individual, diocese, or province holds supremacy over others. The Archbishop of Canterbury is first among equals, *primus inter pares*. Given this institutional relationship, there is considerable potential for a covenantally shaped community of faith. Unfortunately, some Anglicans hold tenaciously to legalistic notions of communion. They subjugate the covenantal ethic to the legalisms of the Anglican formularies—Prayer Book, Ordinal, and the Thirty-nine Articles.[10]

The concept of a communion implies that relationships are governed not by a legalistic mentality but by the ability to find unity in diversity. This unity cannot be legislated. In this covenantal community of faith, the ethical imperative is not to bring persons under subjugation but to share in God's self-emptying love. This was emphasized by Rowan Williams in his address to the 1988 Lambeth conference.

> In the Church's life, we are not to look for a criterion of authority divorced from the pattern of lives transformed; and a Church which could claim impeccable credentials for imparting authoritative information about the sources of the Christian enterprise, but had no capacity to speak or act with conviction for the sake of

the world's liberation would not be sharing in the *exousia* of Jesus.[11]

In the sacraments of Baptism and Eucharist, the *exousia* (authority) of Jesus is combined with an emancipatory praxis. These sacraments symbolize a covenantal ethic of grace, promise, and transformation. In these sacraments, all who acknowledge Jesus Christ as Savior are invited into the mystery of God's self-emptying love in Christ Jesus. Seen in this light, the rite of confirmation is an anachronism that perpetuates a contractarian ethic of duties, qualifications, and conditions to be met before one is permitted to participate fully in the mystery of the Holy Eucharist.

The ethic of grace and transformation needs to be reaffirmed in critical areas of Anglicanism, especially in regard to the ordination of women, the empowerment of the laity, and the promotion of cultural diversity. Two women are presently serving as bishops in the Anglican Communion; one in the United States as a suffragan in Massachusetts, the other as a diocesan in New Zealand. The time is fast approaching for the last bastions of patriarchy in the Anglican Communion to fall like the Berlin Wall. The empowerment of the laity is inseparable from the issue of patriarchy. The recovery of the laity as the whole people of God cannot be accomplished without new models of clerical leadership that reflect the inclusiveness of God's creation.[12] The same applies to cultural diversity. Anglicans from the margins of the British colonial empire are rapidly outnumbering those in the Church of England. In these and other critical areas, the Anglican Communion is being challenged to rethink the theological and ethical basis of its claims to unity.

Some church leaders are already trying to escape the strenuousness of this enterprise by urging the entire Anglican Communion to surrender to papal authority. They feel that the Anglican Communion is departing from its biblical foundations in responding to the legitimate moral claims of women. Using specious arguments from Pauline theology and illogical deductions from the absence of women from among the first twelve apostles, they insist that God does not call women to ordination to the priesthood. In short, they hold the mystery of

God's revelation hostage to canonical legalisms. And yet, the vitality of the Church as a people of the Way depends on its excitement and passion for new life as more and more of God's creatures find fulfillment in surrendering to God's self-emptying love. The eschatological hope of the people of the Way is that God is not yet finished making all things new. Despite the fact that death has been conquered and the doors of the tomb have been rolled away, some of us still want to return the risen Christ to the grave. If we believe that Emmanuel, "God with us," is still with us and is making all things new, then we place ourselves in the risky position of watching our most cherished defenses against change torpedoed by God, who chose some of the strangest and weakest of mortals to share in God's self-emptying love.

In a word, the retrieval of covenantal theology and ethics is foundational to the task of being formed in the likeness of Christ. A covenanting community of faith is an open community of faith, in that the God with whom it is in covenant is conceived of in terms of temporality and change, always creating, making all things new. What makes the body of Christ such a powerful metaphor of a covenanting community is not its cohesiveness but its vulnerability. In the body of Christ, we discover that the kenotic character of covenanting runs contrary to territorial or ideological defensiveness. Hence, we risk emptying ourselves in response to God's self-emptying love. We see this in the story of Cornelius the centurion, who changed the status quo for all who were excluded from the Way on the basis of ethnic impurity (Acts 10:1-48).

It is unfortunate that the modern Church has all but lost its primordial identity as a people of the Way, a community of learners and followers moving with a God whose Incarnation made concrete an involvement in temporality and change. The movement of the people is not an aimless wandering. It is a process of conversion, set within an ethical and theological framework of covenant. Hearts are turned to God in repentance as new contradictions emerge within ourselves and in the changing circumstances of the world. The people of the Way are apostles as well as disciples. They are sent out into the world as bearers of God's love. To be effective apostles, the people of the

Way have to be able to risk being changed by the world, even to the point of losing faith in God and the ability to love as God loves.[13]

The ethical and theological imperatives of covenant are not grafted in a set of deontological rules and regulations but are embodied in God's redemptive love. This is what makes it possible for us to forgive ourselves and one another. Without forgiveness, we remain stuck in our tracks and are unable to forge new pathways for sharing God's redemptive love. This is what Kierkegaard means when he refers to faith as a "happy passion." It is both a joy and a risk—a joy in that we are called by God, whose faithfulness is eternal; a risk in that everything is up for grabs, every idea, every doctrine, yes, even our lives.

RISKING CHRIST

To suggest that Christian discipleship is a risky business will probably not endear me to those who see it as a bulwark against moral and spiritual ambiguity. Nevertheless, I believe that the resurrected Christ will not take us back to the tomb in order to protect us from the demands of life. The resurrected Christ risked re-entering a world that he himself had changed. This retaking of the world, this repetition, is the heart of Christian faith. This repetition orients us to the future. But what kind of a future?

Kierkegaard makes it clear that the Hegelian diachronic evolution of history, or any such speculation on the continuous development of human culture, civilization, or ideas, goes against the leap of faith found in the life of Christ. In a culture driven by the idea of progress, it is very easy to define the relationship between Christ and culture in terms of this idea.

H. Richard Niebuhr has outlined a typology of the relationship between Christ and culture that is relevant to this discussion.[14] A thorough discussion of Niebuhr's typology is not necessary at this time. I would like to draw attention to his "conversionist" paradigm—Christ the transformer of culture. Foremost is God's redemptive action in history—God's continuing transformation of creation in the Incarnation, death, and

Resurrection of Christ. Christ is not made spiritual and removed from history, for history is the locus of God's action in Jesus the Christ and our responses to this action.

The operative question for Niebuhr is, What is going on? What is God doing? It presupposes trust and loyalty to God, whose faithfulness and trustworthiness are revealed in the biblical history of covenant. The conversionist paradigm is about risking Christ in a world in which more and more strangers to the household (*oikos*) of God from the margins of history are interacting with persons who have claimed a position at the center of the universe. The test of responsible Christian discipleship is the ability to allow our relationships with one another to become a collective response to God's invitation to covenantal living. The conversionist paradigm is oriented to the future. It affirms that with God all things are possible and that all creation risks being changed in the image of God and to the glory of God.[15]

Niebuhr distinguishes between Christianity as transformer of culture, for example in Augustine's theology, and F. D. Maurice's view of the kingdom of God as transformed culture that begins in human hearts and permeates social life. He declares his affinity with Maurice. For both of them, the conversion of hearts to Christ spills over into a widening nexus of interpersonal relations and social action. Risking Christ means holding on to radical monotheistic faith but letting go of the prejudices that impede God's transformation of the world.

And so, as the Church faces the reality of its identity as a people of the Way, it risks being changed by those who join its pilgrimage. This is dramatically presented in Luke's account of the post-Resurrection conversation along the way to Emmaus (Luke 24:13-35). Disciples of Christ risk being joined in their journey of faith by the resurrected Christ. At least we should have the humility to admit our blindness and ignorance, even when we are sure of where we are going. As in the Emmaus narrative, the new life given by the resurrected Christ has to be reincarnated in new ways and new circumstances from generation to generation. That the eyes of the disciples were opened during the breaking of the bread reaffirms for me the importance of the sacrament of holy Eucharist as a perpetual celebration of God's transformation of history.

I am suggesting, therefore, that the conversionist paradigm fits the sacramental tradition of Anglicanism, inherent in which is an emancipatory praxis that is informed by the *kenosis* of Christ. Without this kenotic praxis, the various orders of the Church's ministry would degenerate into static forms of power. The paradox in Paul's kenotic hymn is that Christ acceded to his power not by pulling rank ("equality with God") but by becoming "obedient to the point of death—even death on a cross."

CONCLUSION

Let me summarize what I consider to be the essential requirements of a kenotic emancipatory praxis. First, it requires obedience to God. Paul reminds us that Christ was obedient unto death, "even death on a cross." Regrettably, obedience is commonly understood as subjugation to authority. I suggest that we recover for Christian discipleship the etymological roots of obedience as the ability to *listen* (from the Latin *audire*) as a prerequisite of responding to the will of God. Christ's obedience unto death was not a unidimensional abdication of power but a multidimensional action of listening and responding, fulfillment and emptiness.

Second, a kenotic emancipatory praxis in Christian discipleship includes a trinitarian understanding of God's self-emptying love in the work of the Holy Spirit. Like the wind, the Holy Spirit "bloweth where it listeth." We cannot cling to its power. Listening to the Holy Spirit might very well mean risking and surrendering cherished positions of power and authority for the sake of Christ.

Third, a kenotic emancipatory praxis breaks open the conclaves of power to the powerless. The paradox of power in a kenotic emancipatory praxis is that power finds its true meaning in God's self-emptying love and compassion.[16] As we find ourselves up against structures and situations of domination and oppression, Niebuhr's question, What is going on? is most pertinent. Are we allowing God's redemptive and self-emptying love to create new opportunities for service to God and one another, or have we foreclosed on God's ability to make all things new? How do we perpetuate the reincarnation of God's self-emptying love in the midst of human degradation?

In the United States and Canada, any response that ignores the history of racism is entirely unsatisfactory. Canada has always basked in the heroic light of its historical location at the end of the underground railroad, and is proud of its role as a refuge for the oppressed and as international peacekeeper. But one has only to look at the horrible conditions under which its aboriginal peoples exist on the reservations, and the treachery of the Europeans in failing to live up to treaties, by robbing the natives of their land and suppressing their legitimate claims by military domination, to be reminded of the reality. The noble myth of multiculturalism is meant to signal a clear commitment to cultural diversity. Supposedly, it lacks the crudeness of the American melting pot. It does not take much research into Canadian history to discover that multiculturalism is a thin veil that is incapable of concealing vicious intolerance of linguistic and ethnic diversity.

In this frightening vortex of power and powerlessness, the Church is under pressure to witness to Christ's transforming presence in the world. Communities of faith are struggling to enter deeply into the suffering of the world.

> If we are to mirror God, to be in God's image, to invite God to indwell us so that we live Christ's life in today's world, we have to be willing to enter our individual wounds and through them the wounds of the community. We have to be willing to enter the wound of history, particularly the wound of Judeo-Christian history. We have to be willing to enter the wound of God. We have to be willing to enter these wounds, not hide them by casuistry, not seal them up, not scar them over. They must remain wounds in order that Christ's resurrection may enter and indwell us and our wounds be united and glorified with his. This is the way of transfiguration, which is an ongoing process, both within the arrow of time and outside of time's illusion.[17]

Maggie Ross makes it very clear that "we *do* in fact have the criterion we need, and that is the humility of Christ" for entering into the "wound of history."[18] In Jesus' cry of dereliction we hear the cries of all who suffer. A kenotic emancipatory praxis shifts the focus of attention away from the self and toward God. But this is a mutual *kenosis*, since God's self-emptying love is directed toward all of God's creatures. We enter into the pain of God and God enters into our pain. This is neither an exercise in religious privatism nor a basis for religious triumphalism. On the contrary, mutual *kenosis* is the heart of a people called by God to form genuine covenantal and compassionate relationships in a fragmented world. This is the vocation of the local church.

> The plight and the hope of the world are not entirely concealed in other forms of social grouping, but the idiom of the congregational household often expresses for Christians most persistently and poignantly God's call and the human cry.
> Servants belong to households. When Christ emptied himself, he took the form not only of a servant but also of the household that bound his servanthood. That house was at once the *oikoumenē*, the whole inhabited world, and all local households, all homely, and all served by the house servant Christ in their limited but imaginative form.[19]

The *kenosis* of God in Christ models for women and men the moral imagination necessary for solidarity with victims, and the religious imagination necessary for entering into the mystery of God's self-giving love.

NOTES

INTRODUCTION

1. A. David Napier, *Masks, Transformation, and Paradox* (Berkeley: University of California Press, 1986).
2. Tom Driver, *Christ in a Changing World* (New York: Crossroad, 1981).

1. RELIGIOUS FAITH AND THE MORAL LIFE

1. Martin Marty, *The Public Church* (New York: Crossroad, 1981).
2. Parker Palmer, *A Company of Strangers* (New York: Crossroad, 1981).
3. Robert Bellah, et al., *Habits of the Heart* (Berkeley: University of California, 1985).
4. William James, *The Varieties of Religious Experience* (New York: Macmillan, 1902, 1961), p. 42. Hereafter referred to as *Varieties.*
5. Ibid., p. 220.
6. Ibid., pp. 194, 198.
7. Henry S. Levenson, *The Religious Investigations of William James* (Chapel Hill, N.C.: University of North Carolina Press, 1981), p. 115. *See also* Peter Slater, *The Dynamics of Religion: Meaning and Change in Religious Traditions* (New York: Harper & Row, Publishers, 1978), pp. 113-33.
8. William James, *Principles of Psychology, I* (New York: Holt, 1890, 1950), p. 297. Hereafter referred to as *Principles, I.*
9. John Wild, *The Radical Empiricism of William James* (New York: Doubleday Anchor, 1970), p. 85.
10. William James, "The Moral Philosopher and Moral Life," in *The Will to Believe, and Other Essays in Popular Philosophy: Human Immortality* (New York: Dover Publications, 1956), p. 211. Hereafter referred to as *WTB.*
11. Ibid., p. 213.
12. Don Browning, *Pluralism and Personality* (London and Toronto: Associated University Presses, 1980), p. 28. Lewis Rambo offers a more concise

interpretation of the strenuous life in his paper, "Evolution, Community, and the Strenuous Life: The Context of William James' *Varieties of Religious Experience*, presented at the American Academy of Religion, Annual Meeting, December 31, 1977.

13. *WTB*, pp. 212-13.
14. *Varieties*, p. 140.
15. James, "The Energies of Men," *Philosophical Review* 16 (January 1907): 1-20. *Pragmatism: A New Name for Some Old Ways of Thinking* (New York and London: Longmans, Green, and Co., 1907). *A Pluralistic Universe* (New York and London: Longmans, Green, and Co., 1909).
16. *See* George M. Beard, *American Nervousness* (1881). *See also* reference in Bellah et al., *Habits of the Heart*, pp. 116-17.
17. *WTB*, p. 262.
18. *Memories and Studies* (New York and London: Longmans, Green, and Co., 1911), 8 vols., pp. 280-81.
19. *See* Howard M. Feinstein, *Becoming William James* (New York: Cornell University Press, 1984).
20. William James, "Pragmatism and Radical Empiricism," in John J. McDermott, *The Writings of William James* (New York: Random House, Modern Library, 1967), p. 341.
21. *Varieties*, pp. 399-400.
22. Ibid.
23. William James, *Essays in Radical Empiricism, A Pluralistic Universe* (Gloucester, Mass.: Peter Smith, 1967), p. 44. Hereafter referred to as *Essays*.
24. *Varieties*, p. 108.
25. Ibid.
26. *Essays*, pp. 31-32.
27. Ibid., pp. 321-22. *See also* Levenson, *Religious Investigations*, pp. 240-69, and William J. Everett, *God's Federal Republic* (New York: Paulist Press, 1988).
28. Paul expresses similar views on divine-human cooperation in II Cor. 6:1 and I Cor. 3:9.
29. *Varieties*, p. 220.
30. Ibid., p. 42.
31. Ibid., p. 24.
32. Ibid., pp. 220-21.
33. Ibid.
34. Ibid., p. 287.
35. Ibid., p. 45.
36. William James, *Pragmatism and the Meaning of Truth*, Intro. A. J. Ayer (Cambridge: Harvard University Press, 1978), p. 140.
37. *WTB*, pp. 61-62.

2. DEVELOPMENTAL TRANSFORMATIONS

1. Lawrence Kohlberg, "Appendix A: The Six Stages of Justice Development," in *Essays on Moral Development*, vol. 2 (San Francisco: Harper & Row, Publishers, 1984), pp. 621-39.
2. James W. Fowler, *Stages of Faith* (San Francisco: Harper & Row, Publishers, 1981).
3. H. Richard Niebuhr, *Radical Monotheism and Western Culture* (New York: Harper & Row, Publishers, 1970), pp. 100-113.

4. Wilfred Cantwell Smith, *The Meaning and End of Religion* (New York: Harper & Row, Publishers, 1978).

5. Wilfred Cantwell Smith, *Faith and Belief* (Princeton: Princeton University Press, 1979).

6. Fowler, *Stages of Faith*, p. 276.

7. George Herbert Mead, *Mind, Self, and Society*, ed. and intro. Charles W. Morris (Chicago: University of Chicago Press, 1934).

8. There are significant differences between James, Dewey, Mead, and Niebuhr, a discussion of which is beyond the scope of this study. Nevertheless, the pragmatist influences on Niebuhr are well documented. *See*, e.g., Olga Cravens Hutchingson, *Pragmatic Elements in the Moral Decision-Making of Christian Community: A Study in the Ethics of H. Richard Niebuhr and Paul Lehmann* (Ph.D. dissertation, Emory University, Ann Arbor University Microfilms, 1981); and Israel Scheffler, *Four Pragmatists: A Critical Introduction to Peirce, James, Mead, and Dewey* (London: Routledge and Kegan Paul, 1986).

9. Erik H. Erikson, *The Life Cycle Completed: A Review* (New York: W. W. Norton & Co., 1982), p. 88.

10. Jean Piaget, *Six Psychological Studies* (New York: Random House, Vintage Books, 1967).

11. Marx Wartofsky, "From Praxis to Logos: Genetic Psychology and Physics," in T. Mischel, ed., *Cognitive Development and Epistemology* (New York: Academic Press, 1971), p. 135.

12. Douglas John Hall, *Imaging God: Dominion as Stewardship* (Grand Rapids, Mich.: Wm. B. Eerdmans, Friendship Press, 1986), p. 125.

13. Romney M. Moseley, "Faith Development and Conversion in the Catechumenate," in Robert Duggan, ed., *Conversion and the Catechumenate* (New York: Paulist Press, 1984), p. 154.

14. Romney M. Moseley, David Jarvis, and James Fowler, *Manual for Faith Development Research* (Atlanta: Center for Research in Faith and Moral Development, Candler School of Theology, Emory University, 1986).

15. Erik Erikson, *Identity, Youth, and Crisis* (New York: W. W. Norton & Co., 1968), p. 156.

16. David Tracy, *The Analogical Imagination* (New York: Crossroad, 1981), p. 371.

17. Fowler, *Stages of Faith*, p. 198.

18. James W. Fowler, "Faith and the Structuring of Meaning" in Craig Dykstra and Sharon Parks, eds., *Faith Development and Fowler* (Birmingham: Religious Education Press, 1986), pp. 23-24.

19. Sallie McFague, *Models of God: Theology for an Ecological Nuclear Age* (Philadelphia: Fortress Press, 1987), p. 33. McFague's views on metaphor are similar to Ricoeur's. *See* Paul Ricoeur, *The Rule of Metaphor: Multidisciplinary Studies in the Creation of Meaning in Language*, trans. Robert Czerny with Kathleen McLaughlin and John Costello, S. J. (London: Routledge and Kegan Paul, 1978). For an in-depth study of the Ricoeurian implications of metaphor and symbol in faith development theory, *see* Heinz Streib-Weickum, *Hermeneutics of Metaphor, Symbol and Narrative in Faith Development Theory* (Ph.D. dissertation, Emory University, 1989).

20. *See* Howard Slaatte, *The Paradox of Existentialist Theology* (New York: Humanities Press, 1971).

21. McFague, *Models of God*, p. 32.

22. Ibid., p. 35.

23. For a critical study of the function of the imagination in faith development, *see* Sharon Parks, "Imagination and Spirit in Faith Development: A Way Past the Structure-Content Dichotomy," in Dykstra and Parks, eds., *Faith Development and Fowler*, pp. 136-56.

24. Garrett Green, *Imagining God: Theology and the Religious Imagination* (San Francisco: Harper & Row, Publishers, 1989), pp. 54-55.

25. Ibid., p. 53.

26. Janet Martin Soskice, *Metaphor and Religious Language* (Oxford: Clarendon Press, 1985), p. 148.

3. DIALECTICAL TRANSFORMATIONS

1. For example, Klaus Riegel, *Foundations of Dialectical Psychology* (New York: Academic Press, 1979); Allan Buss, *A Dialectical Psychology* (New York: Irvington Publications, 1979).

2. John Broughton, "Piaget's Structural Developmental Psychology, I-V, *Human Development* 24 (1981): 389.

3. Robert Kegan, *The Evolving Self* (Cambridge: Harvard University Press, 1982).

4. James W. Fowler, "Faith and the Structuring of Meaning," in C. Dykstra and S. Parks, *Faith Development and Fowler* (Birmingham: Religious Education Press, 1986), p. 23.

5. Romney M. Moseley, "Religious Conversion: A Structural-Developmental Analysis" (Ph.D. dissertation, Harvard University, 1978).

6. For a sociological analysis of this cultural phenomenon, *see* Steven M. Tipton, *Getting Saved from the Sixties* (Berkeley: University of California Press, 1982).

7. For example, John M. Hull, *What Prevents Adults from Learning?* (London: SCM, 1985).

8. Søren Kierkegaard, *The Sickness Unto Death*, ed. and trans. with Introduction and Notes by Howard V. Hong and Edna H. Hong (Princeton: Princeton University Press, 1980), p. 79.

9. Søren Kierkegaard, *Either/Or*, vol. 1, trans. David Swenson and Lilian M. Swenson (Princeton: Princeton University Press, 1959), p. 354.

10. Stephen Toulmin, "The Concept of Stage in Piaget's Theory," in T. Mischel, ed., *Cognitive Development and Epistemology* (New York: Academic Press, 1971), p. 46.

11. Ibid.

12. Ibid., p. 52.

13. Ibid., p. 54.

14. H. Richard Niebuhr, *Christ and Culture* (New York: Harper & Row, Publishers, 1956), pp. 244-45.

15. Carol Gilligan, *In a Different Voice: Psychological Theory and Women's Development* (Cambridge: Harvard University Press, 1982).

16. William Julius Wilson, *The Truly Disadvantaged: The Inner City, the Underclass, and Public Policy* (Chicago: University of Chicago Press, 1987).

17. Matthew Lamb, "The Dialectics of Theory and Praxis Within Paradigm Analysis," in Hans Küng and David Tracy, eds., *Paradigm Change in Theology* (New York: Crossroad, 1989), pp. 97-98.

4. ARCHETYPAL TRANSFORMATIONS

1. C. G. Jung, *The Collected Works of C. G. Jung*, trans. R. F. C. Hull, ed. H. Read, M. Fordham, G. Adler, W. McGuire, Bollingen Series XX (Princeton: Princeton University Press, 1953–1979), vol. 5, par. 351. Hereafter referred to as *CW*.
2. Karl Plank, *Paul and the Irony of Affliction* (Atlanta: Scholars Press, 1987), p. 64.
3. Ibid.
4. *See* Naomi Goldenberg, *The Changing of the Gods* (New York: Beacon Press, 1979); *The End of God* (Ottawa: University of Ottawa, 1982); Demaris Wehr, *Jung and Feminism* (Boston: Beacon Press, 1987); Catherine Keller, *From a Broken Web: Separation, Sexism, and Self* (Boston: Beacon Press, 1986).
5. *See* Sylvia Brinton Perera, "The Descent of Inanna: Myth and Therapy" in Estella Lauter and Carol Schreiter Rupprecht, eds., *Feminist Archetypal Theory: Interdisciplinary Re-Visions of Jungian Thought* (Knoxville, Tenn.: University of Tennessee Press, 1985), pp. 137-86. Note Perera's interest in the internal coherence of the image of the goddess as Self.
6. *See* Emma Jung, *Animus and Anima* (Zürich: Spring Publications, 1974).
7. Episcopal Bishop John Spong argues the case for homosexuality as a biological phenomenon. *See Living in Sin? A Bishop Rethinks Human Sexuality* (New York: Harper & Row, Publishers, 1989). Similarly, William Countryman feels that the church should bless homosexual relationships as it does marriages. *See* William Countryman, *Dirt, Greed, and Sex* (Philadelphia: Fortress Press, 1988).
8. *See* Sallie McFague, *Models of God: Theology for an Ecological, Nuclear Age* (Philadelphia: Fortress Press, 1987). McFague explores images of God as lover, friend, mother, judge, healer, and liberator as alternatives to the classical, hierarchical, and monarchical model of God. McFague's models reflect the wholeness of creation and the interdependence of humanity and the ecosystem.
9. Aniela Jaffe, *The Myth of Meaning in the Work of C. G. Jung* (Zürich: Daimon Verlag, 1984), p. 21.
10. Jung's ideas reflect the influence of Rudolf Otto's classical work, *The Idea of the Holy*, trans. J. W. Harvey (London: Oxford University Press, 1923).
11. Jung, "The Undiscovered Self" in *Civilization in Transition*, CW, 10, par. 565.
12. Jung, *Answer to Job*, CW, vol. 11.
13. *See* Jung, *Memories, Dreams, Reflections*, trans. Aniela Jaffe (New York: Vintage Books, 1965). Note Jung's vision of feces dropping on the cathedral in Basel.
14. CW, 9 *(Aion)*, part 2, par. 38.
15. Liliane Frey-Rohn, "The Psychological View" in *Evil* (Zürich: C. G. Jung Institute and Northwestern University, 1967), p. 183.
16. Jung, *Psychology and Religion*, CW, 11, "A Psychological Approach to the Dogma of the Trinity," par. 254.
17. Jung, *Psychology and Religion*, CW, 11, par. 97.
18. Jung, *Aion*, CW, 9, par. 49.
19. *See* Anthony Stevens, *Archetypes* (New York: Quill, 1983), p. 178; Erich Neumann, *The Great Mother, An Analysis of the Archetype* (London: Routledge and Kegan Paul, 1955). Jung considered the doctrine of the Assumption of Mary an effort on the part of the Roman Catholic Church to respond to the completion *(teleiosis)* of the quaternity.

20. Robert Doran, *Theology and the Dialectics of History* (Toronto: University of Toronto Press, 1990), p. 272.

21. Ibid., p. 273.

22. *See* Gilles Quispel, "C. G. Jung und die Gnosis," in *Eranos Jahrbuch 1968* (Zürich, 1969), pp. 227ff.

23. Garrett Green, *Imagining God: Theology and the Religious Imagination* (San Francisco: Harper & Row, Publishers, 1989), p. 102.

24. John Skorupski, *Symbol and Theory* (Cambridge: Cambridge University Press, 1976), pp. 216-17.

25. Doran, *Dialectics of History*, p. 272.

26. Ibid.

27. Brian Hebblethwaite, "MacKinnon and the Problem of Evil" in Kenneth Surin, ed., *Christ, Ethics, and Tragedy* (Cambridge: Cambridge University Press, 1989), p. 142.

28. Erich Neumann, *Depth Psychology and a New Ethic* (New York: Harper & Row, Publishers, 1973), p. 146.

29. Plank, *Irony of Affliction*, p. 31.

5. BECOMING A SELF BEFORE GOD

1. Søren Kierkegaard, *The Sickness unto Death*, ed. and trans. Howard V. Hong and Edna H. Hong, with introduction and notes (Princeton: Princeton University Press, 1980), p. 50. Hereafter referred to as SUD. For secondary literature on Kierkegaard's concept of the self, *see* J. Preston Cole, *The Problematic Self in Kierkegaard and Freud* (New Haven: Yale University Press, 1971); John H. Smith, ed., *Kierkegaard's Truth: The Disclosure of the Self* (New Haven: Yale University Press, 1981); Mark Taylor, *Journeys to Selfhood: Hegel and Kierkegaard* (Berkeley: University of California Press, 1980).

2. SUD, p. 51.

3. Ibid.

4. Ibid., p. 20.

5. Ibid., p. 15.

6. Ibid., p. 72.

7. Søren Kierkegaard, *Fear and Trembling/Repetition*, ed. and trans. Howard V. Hong and Edna H. Hong, with introduction and notes (Princeton: Princeton University Press, 1983), p. 275. Hereafter referred to as F/R.

8. F/R, pp. 131-32.

9. Ibid., p. 322.

10. Ibid., p. 149.

11. Ibid., p. 132.

12. Ibid., p. 136.

13. Ibid., p. 137.

14. SUD, p. 38.

15. F/R, p. 327.

16. Søren Kierkegaard, *Either/Or*, vol. 2, trans. W. Lowrie, revisions by H. Johnson (Princeton: Princeton University Press, 1972), p. 354. Hereafter referred to as E/O.

17. *See* Søren Kierkegaard, *Concluding Unscientific Postscript*, Trans. David Swenson and Walter Lowrie (Princeton: Princeton University Press, 1941), pp. 474-75. Hereafter referred to as CUP.

18. Abrahim Khan, *Salighed as Happiness?* (Waterloo: Wilfred Laurier University Press, 1985), p. 46.

19. Ibid.
20. Ibid.
21. *See* John Elrod, *Being and Existence in Kierkegaard's Pseudonymous Authorship* (Princeton: Princeton University Press, 1975).
22. Khan, *Salighed,* p. 52.
23. Ibid.
24. Ibid., p. 53.
25. E/O, 1, p. 292.
26. SUD, p. 80.
27. E/O, 2, p. 181.
28. Krister Stendahl, *Paul Among the Jews and Gentiles* (Philadelphia: Fortress Press, 1976), p. 7.
29. Beverly Roberts Gaventa, *From Darkness to Light: Aspects of Conversion in the New Testament* (Philadelphia: Fortress Press, 1986), p. 3.
30. Ibid., p. 42.
31. Ibid., p. 43.
32. Ibid., p. 40.
33. Ibid.
34. Ibid.
35. Thomas Kuhn, *The Structure of Scientific Revolutions* (Chicago: University of Chicago Press, 1970).
36. Gaventa, *Darkness,* p. 45.
37. *See,* e.g., the recently published extensive study by Alan Segal, *Paul the Convert* (New Haven: Yale University Press, 1990).
38. Søren Kierkegaard, *Philosophical Fragments,* trans. David Swenson, rev. Howard V. Hong (Princeton: Princeton University Press, 1967), p. 18. Hereafter referred to as PF.
39. Ibid., p. 19.
40. Ibid.
41. E/O, 1, p. 165.
42. Marvin C. Shaw, *The Paradox of Intention* (Atlanta: Scholars Press, 1988).
43. CUP, p. 507.
44. *See* Søren Kierkegaard, *Training in Christianity,* trans. with Introduction and Notes by Walter Lowrie (Princeton: Princeton University Press, 1967).
45. Mark Taylor, *Journeys to Selfhood: Hegel and Kierkegaard* (Berkeley: University of California Press, 1980), p. 257.
46. Taylor, *Journeys,* pp. 258-59.
47. E/O, 1, p. 215.
48. CUP, p. 506.

6. KENOTIC TRANSFORMATIONS

1. Richard Bondi, *Leading God's People: Ethics for the Practice of Ministry* (Nashville: Abingdon Press, 1989), p. 60.
2. *See* Gottfried Thomasius, *Beitrage zur kirklichen Christologie* (Erlangen, 1845) and *Christi Person und Werk* (Erlangen, 1853). English trans. of both works in Claude Welch, ed., *God and Incarnation in Mid-Nineteenth Century German Theology* (New York: Oxford University Press, 1965).
3. Note also Thomasius' distinction between absolute power and omnipotence. The latter is "the activation of absolute power on the finite." Absolute power

is "the unconditioned power of will over itself, thus wholly in the service of will (and susceptible of self-limitation)" in Welch, *God and Incarnation*, p. 69, n. 10.

4. Lucien Richard, O. M. I., *A Kenotic Christology* (Lanham, Md.: University Press of America, 1982), p. 159.
5. Ibid., p. 160.
6. Welch, *God and Incarnation*, p. 66.
7. John Macquarrie, "Kenoticism Reconsidered," The Charles Gore Memorial Lecture, St. Margaret's, Westminster, November 6, 1973, *Theology* 77 (March 1974): 121.
8. Ibid., p. 122. *See also* Wolfhart Pannenberg, *Jesus—God and Man* (Philadelphia: Westminster Press, 1968), p. 279.
9. Macquarrie, "Kenoticism Reconsidered," p. 123.
10. Ibid.
11. Matthew Lamb, *Solidarity with Victims: Toward a Theology of Social Transformation* (New York: Crossroad, 1982), p. ix.
12. SUD, pp. 29ff.
13. Paulo Freire, *Pedagogy of the Oppressed*, trans. Myra Bergman Ramos (London: Penguin Books, 1972).
14. Louis Mackey, *Points of View: Readings of Kierkegaard* (Tallahassee, Fl.: Florida State University Press, 1986), p. 122.
15. Douglas John Hall, *God and Human Suffering* (Minneapolis: Augsburg, 1986).
16. Kazoh Kitamori, *Theology of the Pain of God* (Philadelphia: Westminster Press, 1965), p. 22.
17. Gustavo Gutiérrez, *On Job* (Maryknoll, N.Y.: Orbis Books, 1989), p. 94. *See also* Juan Luis Segundo, *Our Idea of God* (Maryknoll, N.Y.: Orbis Books, 1974).
18. Delwin Brown, "Thinking About the God of the Poor: Questions for Liberation Theology from Process Thought," *Journal of the American Academy of Religion* 57 (Summer 1989): 273.
19. Ibid., p. 275.
20. Ibid., p. 276.
21. Ibid., p. 277.
22. Ibid., p. 276.
23. Ibid., p. 278.
24. H. Richard Niebuhr, *The Responsible Self* (San Francisco: Harper & Row, Publishers, 1963), p. 60.
25. John Cobb, *Process Theology as Political Theology* (Philadelphia: Westminster Press, 1982). Cf. Johannes Metz, *Faith in History and Society*, trans. David Smith (New York: Seabury Press, 1980).
26. Louis Dupre, *Transcendent Selfhood* (New York: Seabury Press, 1976), p. 72.
27. These ideas on kenotic love are also found in G. MacGregor, *He Who Lets Us Be: A Theology of Love* (New York: Seabury Press, 1975); Jean-Marc Laporte, S. J., *Patience and Power: Grace for the First World* (New York: Paulist Press, 1988).

7. LETTING GO, RISKING CHRIST

1. In Matthew Fox, *Meditations on Meister Eckhart* (Santa Fe: Bear & Co., 1982), p. 67.

2. Theodore A. McConnell, "The *Via Media* as Theological Method" in Paul Elmen, ed., *The Anglican Moral Choice* (Wilton, Conn.: Morehouse Barlow, 1983), p. 158.
3. W. Taylor Stevenson, "Lex Orandi–Lex Credendi," in Stephen Sykes and John Booty, eds., *The Study of Anglicanism* (Philadelphia: Fortress Press, 1988), p. 178.
4. Paul Ricoeur, *Freud and Philosophy: An Essay on Interpretation*, trans. D. Savage (New Haven: Yale University Press, 1970), pp. 28-32.
5. Stevenson, "Lex Orandi–Lex Credendi," p. 183.
6. Ibid., p. 185.
7. Thomas W. Ogletree, *Hospitality to the Strangers* (Philadelphia: Fortress Press, 1985), pp. 118-19. *See also* Hans-Georg Gadamer, *Truth and Method*, trans. G. Barden and J. Cumming (New York: Seabury Press, 1975). For an insightful application of Gadamer's hermeneutics to pastoral theology, *see* Charles V. Gerkin, *Widening the Horizons* (Philadelphia: Westminster Press, 1986).
8. Ogletree, *Hospitality to the Strangers,* pp. 118-19.
9. William F. May, "Code, Covenant, Contract, or Philanthropy" in *The Hastings Center Report* 5 (December 1975): 31. *See also* Walter Brueggemann, "Covenanting as Human Vocation: A Discussion of the Relation of Bible and Pastoral Care," *Interpretation* 33, no. 2 (1979): 115-29.
10. For example, *see* W. J. Hankey, "Canon Law" in S. Sykes and J. Booty, eds., *The Study of Anglicanism,* p. 212. A very different view is provided by Arthur Michael Ramsey, the one hundredth Archbishop of Canterbury in his brief essay, "Looking to the Future," in Arthur A. Vogel, ed., *Theology in Anglicanism* (Wilton, Conn.: Morehouse Barlow, 1984), pp. 159-62. Archbishop Ramsey points out that "the Thirty-nine Articles had their significance not as a confessional definition but as an aid to the recovery of the scriptural and primitive faith, a recovery which indeed demanded the saying Yea or Nay to some of the controversial positions of the time."
11. In V. Samuel and C. Sugden, eds., *Lambeth,* p. 111.
12. Frederica Harris Thompsett, "The Laity," in S. Sykes and J. Booty, eds., *The Study of Anglicanism,* pp. 245-60; Verna Dozier, *The Authority of the Laity* (Washington, D.C.: Alban Institute, 1982).
13. *See* Roberta C. Bondi, *To Love as God Loves* (Philadelphia: Fortress Press, 1987).
14. H. Richard Niebuhr, *Christ and Culture* (New York: Harper & Row, Publishers, 1951).
15. *See* M. M. Thomas, *Risking Christ for Christ's Sake* (Geneva: World Council of Churches Publications, 1987).
16. *See* C. S. Song, *The Compassionate God* (Maryknoll, N.Y.: Orbis Books, 1982).
17. Maggie Ross, *Pillars of Flame: Power, Priesthood, and Spiritual Maturity* (San Francisco: Harper & Row, Publishers, 1988), p. xvii.
18. Ibid.
19. James Hopewell, *Congregation: Stories and Structures,* ed. Barbara Wheeler (Philadelphia: Fortress Press, 1987), p. 12.

INDEX

141